100 WA~~
Devon & ~~

compiled by

P L O'Shea
&
B M O'Shea
(plus Goldie & Ash, their *constant* companions)

The Crowood Press

First published in 1996 by
The Crowood Press Ltd
Ramsbury
Marlborough
Wiltshire SN8 2HR

British Library Cataloguing-in-Publication Data
A catalogue record for this book is
available from the British Library

ISBN 1 85223 952 2

All maps by Janet Powell

Typeset by Carreg Limited, Ross-on-Wye, Herefordshire

Printed by J W Arrowsmith Ltd, Bristol

CONTENTS

Devon

37.	Bigbury and Erme Mouth	8m	(13km)
38.	... and longer version	11½m	(18km)
39.	Arlington and Bratton Fleming	8m	(13km)
40.	Hartland Point	8m	(13km)
41.	Bellever and Postbridge	8m	(13km)
42.	Dittisham	8½m	(14km)
43.	Dartmouth Castle and Stoke Fleming	8½m	(14km)
44.	Yarcombe and Stockland	8½m	(14km)
45.	Buckfastleigh Moor and Ryder's Hill	8½m	(14km)
46.	Sidbury	9m	(14½km)
47.	Braunton and Halsinger	9m	(14½km)
48.	Umberleigh and Chittlehampton	9m	(14½km)
49.	Steps Bridge to Mardon Down	9m	(14½km)
50.	Cosdon Beacon and Hound Tor	9½m	(15km)
51.	Two Bridges and Rough Tor	9½m	(15km)
52.	Shipley Bridge and Red Lake	10m	(16km)
53.	North-east Dartmoor	10½m	(17km)
54.	Fur Tor and Tavy Cleave	10½m	(17km)
55.	Corn Ridge and Great Links Tor	11m	(17½km)
56.	Bolt Head and Bolt Tail	11m	(17½km)
57.	Lydford's Forest and Gorge	11m	(17½km)
58.	Countisbury and County Gate	11½m	(18km)

Cornwall

59.	Golitha Falls and Siblyback Reservoir	3m	(5km)
60.	Boscastle Harbour and Valley	3m	(5km)
61.	Gwennap and Porthcurno	3½m	(6km)
62.	... and longer version	6½m	(10km)
63.	St Ewe and Polmassick	4m	(6½km)
64.	Luxulyan Valley and the Saints Way	4m	(6½km)
65.	... and longer version	12m	(19km)
66.	Tintagel	4m	(6½km)
67.	Prussia and Perranuthnoe	4m	(6½km)
68.	Gorran Haven and the Deadman	4½m	(7km)
69.	Holywell and Kelsey Head	4½m	(7km)
70.	Mylor Bridge and Restronguet	4¾m	(7½km)
71.	Looe Pool – The Penrose Walks	5m	(8km)
72.	Porthpean and Black Head	5m	(8km)
73.	Cape Cornwall and the Cot Valley	5m	(8km)
74.	Gunnislake and Chilsworthy	5m	(8km)

75.	Brown Willy and Rough Tor	5½m	(9km)
76.	Camelford and Watergate	5½m	(9km)
77.	Kingsand	6m	(9½km)
78.	... and longer version	12m	(19km)
79.	Land's End	6m	(9½km)
80.	Lizard Point	6m	(9½km)
81.	... and longer version	10m	(16km)
82.	Mullion and Kynance Coves	6m	(9½km)
83.	... and longer version	9½m	(15km)
84.	The Roseland Peninsula	6m	(9½km)
85.	Crackington Haven	6½m	(10km)
86.	Bodinnick and Polruan	6½m	(10km)
87.	Coverack and St Keverne	6½m	(10km)
88.	Mevagissey and Gorran Haven	6½m	(10km)
89.	Bude's Canal and Cliffs	6½m	(10km)
90.	Fowey and Polkerris	7m	(11km)
91.	Minions	7½m	(12km)
92.	Polperro and Looe	8m	(13km)
93.	Botallack and Pendeen	8m	(13km)
94.	Portreath and Coombe	8m	(13km)
95.	Bolventor and Brown Willy	8m	(13km)
96.	Lamorna and St Buryan	8½m	(14km)
97.	Trevose Head	9½m	(15km)
98.	Castle-an-Dinas	11m	(17½km)
99.	Altarnun and Jamaica Inn	11½m	(18km)
100.	Zennor and St Ives	12m	(19km)

Walking in Devon and Cornwall – Special Safety Notes

Cliff walking needs special care – never go too near the edge or cross fences to get better views. Always obey notices about crumbling rocks, diversions etc. The steep ascents and descents add to the physical demands and the time taken to complete a walk.

Moorland and coastal walks are often subject to misty conditions so heed the local weather forecasts and do not attempt such walks in poor visibility.

Some parts of Dartmoor are used as Military Firing Ranges. Check with local newspapers, post-offices, camp-sites etc. before setting off. Never pick up metal or plastic objects, they may have been there 50 years, just waiting. 'It could be you...'

PUBLISHER'S NOTE

We very much hope that you enjoy the routes presented in this book, which has been compiled with the aim of allowing you to explore the area in the best possible way – on foot.

We strongly recommend that you take the relevant map for the area, and for this reason we list the appropriate Ordnance Survey maps for each route. Whilst the details and descriptions given for each walk were accurate at time of writing, the countryside is constantly changing, and a map will be essential if, for any reason, you are unable to follow the given route. It is good practice to carry a map and use it so that you are always aware of your exact location.

We cannot be held responsible if some of the details in the route descriptions are found to be inaccurate, but should be grateful if walkers would advise us of any major alterations. Please note that whenever you are walking in the countryside you are on somebody else's land, and we must stress that you should *always* keep to established rights of way, and *never* cross fences, hedges or other boundaries unless there is a clear crossing point.

Remember the country code:

Enjoy the country and respect its life and work
Guard against all risk of fire
Fasten all gates
Keep dogs under close control
Keep to public footpaths across all farmland
Use gates and stiles to cross field boundaries
Leave all livestock, machinery and crops alone
Take your litter home
Help to keep all water clean
Protect wildlife, plants and trees
Make no unnecessary noise

The walks are listed by length – from approximately 1 to 12 miles – but the amount of time taken will depend on the fitness of the walkers and the time spent exploring any points of interest along the way. Nearly all the walks are circular and most offer recommendations for refreshments.

Good walking.

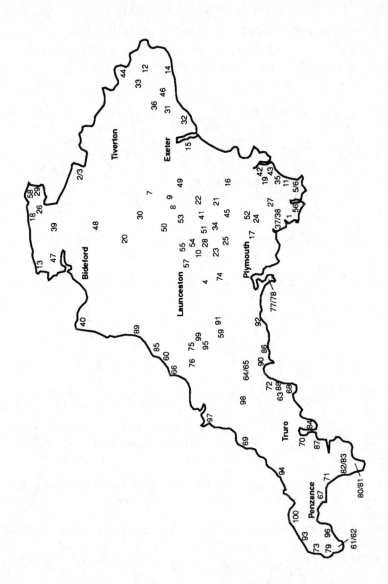

Walk 1   **THURLESTONE AND BANTHAM**   3m (5km)

Maps: OS Sheets Landranger 202; Pathfinder 1362.
A short scenic coastal walk with inland farmland footpaths.
Start: At 673429, All Saints Church, Thurlestone.

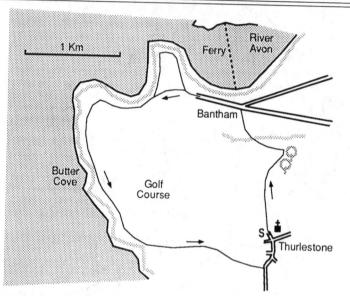

This walk begins in the attractive South Devon Village of **Thurlestone**, by All Saints Church

     Leave the church on the right, going along the gravel path signposted 'Bantham ¹/₂ mile'. Climb the steps to cross a wall and maintain direction across the field beyond to reach a stile. Cross this and, still heading north-westwards, cross two more stiles. Bantham is visible ahead as the path bears right and descends to yet another stile. Cross this and go over a stream. Now, make for the village, bearing left and right across fields, using stiles to cross between them. The path eventually leads just to the right of the inn at Bantham.

     Now turn left, downhill and seawards, going past the car park and public toilets to reach a signed, sandy footpath (Thurlestone, 1 mile). Take this, part of the South West Coastal Path, ascending with excellent channel views. There is a golf course to the left. After a long mile, another sign points inland: follow this path which leads through a gate on to a lane. Turn left and ascend into Thurlestone, soon reaching the church where the walk started.

POINTS OF INTEREST:

Thurlestone – All Saints Church has 13th-century foundations, a Norman font and many other interesting features. The nearby cottages were once a poor house, almshouses and a rector's home. Smuggling was a thriving 'industry' in the 18th and 19th centuries locally: it is said that smuggled spirits were stored in an old house, 'Whiddons', in Bantham and above the church porch here. Spirits were presented to the parson as payment (and some 'baccy for the parish clerk?). The whole village – with its many thatched cottages – deserves an admiring wander.

Thurlestone gets its name from the arched rock offshore, 'thurle' meaning 'hole'.

Bantham – Set at the mouth of the Avon (the Devonian one), the village has a good beach and opportunities for boat trips from the old quay where there are pilchard cellars.

A ferry from Bantham crosses the Avon estuary to Bigbury-on-Sea.

REFRESHMENTS:

The Village Inn, Thurlestone. The inn includes, it is said, timbers from an Armada wreck.

The Sloop Inn, Bantham. The inn has smuggling associations, wood-panelling, a timber-propped ceiling and excellent cuisine.

Walks 2 & 3 ANSTEY GATE AND TARR STEPS 3½m (6km) or 8m (13km)

Maps: OS Sheets Landranger 181; Outdoor Leisure 9.
Two walks in North Devon, straying into Somerset. A taste of Exmoor. Mud perhaps.
Start: At 835298, Anstey Gate.

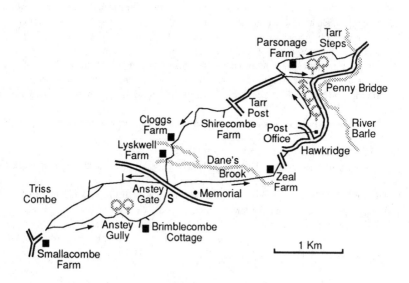

The short walk begins at the car park and heads due west – signposted to 'Molland'. Veer left of the path running parallel to the road and, after a short ¼ mile, cross another path. Ignore the next left path, then go left at a fork, heading south-west, to pass a tree, left. Descend into the combe, heading for fir trees and aim for a farm as the track goes more steeply down. Pass a small quarry, left, and look for a sign 'West Anstey'. Turn left here and ascend, keeping a bank right and a hedge left, to reach the common again: the general direction now is east and the way is undulating to Anstey Gully which drains the common in heavy weather. Continue out of the gully to the entrance to Brimblecombe Cottage. Soon fork uphill, left, to a tall hedge and so back to the start.

The longer walk crosses the road and heads east across Rhiney Moor, passing to the left of the memorial to a stag hunter, making for Zeal Farm. Ignore tracks right or left but take a (muddy) track left on reaching Dane's Brook to cross the stepping stones. (If this is not possible, go downstream to cross Slade Bridge, go left over bridge and up the road. Pass the farm and pick up the route at the road between the Hollowcombe Farms.) At Zeal, go through an iron gate, turn left in front of the farmhouse, go through a white gate, right, down the access road for 50 yards then left, ascending across two fields, to reach a road. Go straight across and make for a solitary tree, turning half-left there to a gate in the field corner. On gaining the road again, go ahead, north eastwards into **Hawkridge**.

Turn left (signposted Withypool) and, just past the Post Office, turn right through a gate. Immediately go left and around two field-edges to another gate. Now keep to the left of four field-edges to reach the entrance road of Parsonage Farm. Turn right down 'Hardway' (signposted 'Tarr Steps') and go down between fir trees, right, and oaks, left, and on reaching the road at Penny Bridge, turn left alongside the river to the clapper bridge, **Tarr Steps**.

After a necessary tarry at Tarr Steps, cross back and fork right up the access road to the hotel. After 80-100 yards, fork right again on to a rough uphill track. Beyond a gate this track becomes sunken, then ascends to a field corner. Follow the hedge to another metal gate, go through and so on to third, fourth and fifth gates. Our way is now through the buildings of Parsonage Farm and so out on to the access road. This goes left over a brook and ascends to a road. Follow this road uphill to Tarr Post. Turn left, but after 50 yards, turn right, pass to the right of Shirecombe Farm and follow red waymarks across fields, over a bridge (Cloggs Farm is off to the right here), then between birch trees, southwards, passing to the left of Lyshwell Farm. Turn right to reach the access road, go over a stream and across the moor to reach the start.

POINTS OF INTEREST:

Hawkridge – The village is high on Exmoor and often isolated in winter snowstorms. The church has a Norman doorway and font.

Tarr Steps – The clapper bridge has been here for more than 700 years, perhaps even since the Bronze Age. The Hotel was once a Rectory.

REFRESHMENTS:

None on the short walk, but Hawkridge and Tarr Steps have cafés.

N.B. Both walks could be accomplished in a day making a figure-of-eight of $11\frac{1}{2}$ miles.

SYDENHAM DAMEREL   4m (6$^1/_2$km)

Maps: OS Sheets Landranger 201; Pathfinder 1340.
A fairly gentle walk, which can be muddy, in the Tamar Valley.
Start: At 409760, Sydenham Damerel.

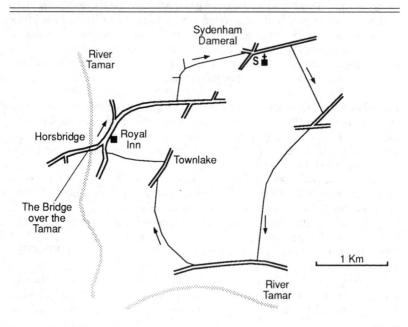

This walk begins in the little hamlet of Sydenham Damerel, which lies on a minor road south of Milton Abbot and north of Gunnislake.

Walk uphill, eastwards, passing the church, on the right. After about 200 yards, turn right along the signed footpath, going along the top of a field. Go through a gate, walk along the top of the next field and go through another gate. Continue along the next field top to reach a stile. Cross and maintain direction to reach a lane. Turn right to soon reach a cross-roads. Do not take the signed footpath on the left: instead, go straight on, walking southwards for almost a mile to reach a T-junction with another quiet lane. Turn right, going uphill along the lane for $^1/_3$ mile to reach a footpath sign in the hedge on the right. Take this footpath, going up steps and then turning left along the field edge to reach a stile in the top corner. Cross and continue along the top of the next field, continuing to reach a track by a gate. Follow the track, heading north-westwards, as it descends to reach a lane. Turn right and follow the lane into the little hamlet of Townlake.

Take the signed footpath on the left, going through a little gate and crossing two fields, linked by two more gates, to reach the lane in the village of **Horsebridge**. Turn right to reach the **Bridge over the Tamar**. The bridge is to your left. Do not cross (but linger for a while): instead, bear right along the road, heading north, to reach the Royal Inn. Continue uphill to reach a road fork. Keep right along the road signed for Sydenham Damerel. As this lane turns to the right, take a track on the left, heading northwards. Follow the track as it bends right and leads back to the starting point.

POINTS OF INTEREST:
Horsebridge – This delightful little village is now 'far from the beaten track' but it cannot always have been so as
The Bridge over the Tamar – was built in 1437, so the settlement here must have been of some importance.

REFRESHMENTS:
The Royal Inn, Horsebridge. This fine inn was once a nunnery.
The Kings Arms, Milton Abbot. Not on route, but close at hand and very good.

START POINT 4¹/₂m (7km)
or 8¹/₂m (14km)

Maps: OS Sheets Landranger 202; Outdoor Leisure 20.
Safe, but strenuous, cliff walking, plus inland paths and lanes.
Start: At 821375, Start Point car park.

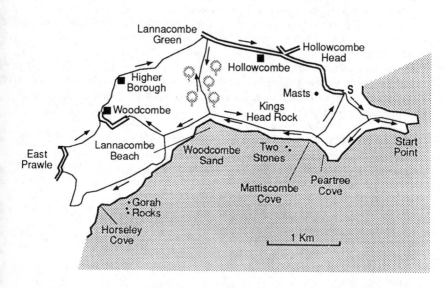

Both walks begin at the car park just short of the Start Point lighthouse.

Descend on the clear path heading south-eastwards. A visit to the automated lighthouse and Start Point itself will add ¹/₂ mile to the walk, the route going past a wooden hut to reach the well-signed **Coastal Path** below the cliffs. Follow the Path past Peartree Cove and Kings Head Rock to Lannacombe Beach. There are steep 'ups and downs', but splendid seascape views all the way. On the beach there is a clear indicator offering an alternative shorter walk by cutting north inland along a pleasant (but sometimes muddy!) little valley. Along this route it is only a short mile to Lannacombe Green, but the 4¹/₂ and 8¹/₂ mile walks continue for a further ¹/₂ mile to reach Woodcombe Sand.

The short walk goes north-westwards here, heading up the valley and across three fields – following the yellow-arrowed signs. On reaching a lane, turn left and soon right to reach the farm buildings of Woodcombe where the longer route is rejoined.

The longer walk continues along the cliffs from Woodcombe Sand for a further short mile – though it may seem longer because of the gradients – to reach the East Prawle signpost at Horseley Cove. Now follow the path steeply up to the village. Continue to the lane junction beyond the Pig's Nose Inn, turning right at the telephone box to follow a track which leads to Woodcombe where the short walk is rejoined.

Continue around three sides of the farm (following blue bridleway marks) and then follow a concrete – becoming gravelly – track northwards to Higher Borough. Again follow the blue markers, keeping to the right at a junction about $^1/_4$ mile further on. Now walk north-eastwards to Lannacombe Green.

At Lannacombe Green it should be possible to see twin wireless masts near the starting point. One way of returning is to follow the lanes due east for $^1/_2$ mile to Hollowcombe Head, then heading south-eastwards for a long mile, passing the masts (to the right) to reach the starting car park.

The more pleasant alternative is to turn southwards at Lannacombe Green, as signed for Lannacombe, and to go down to the beach again. Now go left, reversing the outward route back to the start.

POINTS OF INTEREST:

Coastal Path – The walk follows part of the South Devon Coastal Path, overlooking a part of the English Channel which has seen hundred of shipwrecks. On a pleasant day the Path offers great patches of wild flowers and hundreds of sea birds – gannets, shags and cormorants in particular. It is also a fascinating area for the amateur geologist.

REFRESHMENTS:

The Pig's Nose, East Prawle.
The Grunters Café, East Prawle.

Walk 7   COLEBROOKE $4^1/_2$m (7km)

Maps: OS Sheets Landranger 191; Pathfinder 1294.
Farmland footpaths and quiet lanes plus an excellent inn.
Start: At 770001, Colebrook Church.

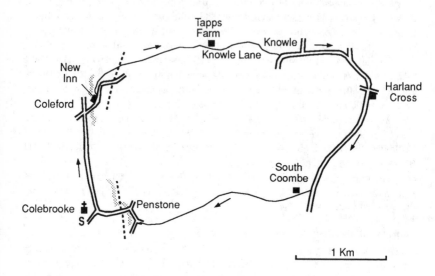

This short walk follows very peaceful farmland footpaths and, for the most part, quiet country lanes. Colebrook is south of the A377. It lies about 4 miles west of Crediton and $2^1/_2$ miles south of Copplestone.

From the church, head north-eastwards at first to reach a lane. Turn left, northwards, along the lane going out of the village, with the railway to the right. After a short $^1/_2$ mile, in the hamlet of Coleford, turn right to reach the New Inn, on the left. Very soon after, go through the iron gate, on the left, by the Coleford road sign. Cross the field beyond to go under a railway line. Now head north-eastwards crossing three stiles and going along field edges. Go over a fourth stile on to Knowle Lane.

Go ahead, eastwards, along the lane, passing Tapps Farm to reach the hamlet of Knowle. There, take the gravelly track which is unsuitable for motors for a further $1/_4$ mile to reach a T-junction. Turn right, southwards, following the road to the crossroads at Harland Cross. Go straight over, still heading southwards, and continue to the top of the hill. Continue downhill for another $1/_2$ mile to reach a turn to the right, the access lane to South Combe Farm.

Take this lane, going through gates at the farm. Maintain direction (westwards), keeping to the left of a large oak tree and going over a little brook. Now keep straight on along a valley, going through gates and descending, with hedges to the right, to Penstone, another little hamlet. When a lane is reached at the hamlet, turn right, then left to pass over the river and under the railway line. Now walk up the hill to Colbrooke Church and the start of the walk.

POINTS OF INTEREST:
There is nothing extra special about this walk, so there is plenty of time to savour the typical Devonian farmland that lies to the north-east of Dartmoor. At the appropriate season there is plenty for the wild flower 'collector' (although the flowers will not be picked!) while birds and bird song feature everywhere.

REFRESHMENTS:
The New Inn, Coleford. Dating from the 13th century and beautifully thatched, the inn has a very well deserved reputation for fine ales and good food.

Walk 8   CHAGFORD AND THE RIVER TEIGN   4$^1/_2$m (7km)

Maps: OS Sheets Landranger 191; Outdoor Leisure 28.

An easy walk through woodland and alongside a river, with a steep climb early on.

Start: At 701875, St Michael's Church, Chagford.

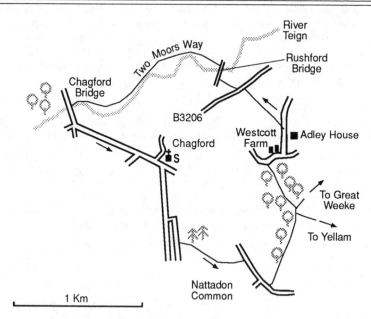

Spend some time exploring **Chagford** before taking the road running southwards and passing many attractive cottages. After 500 yards bear left to reach a signpost for Nattadon Common. Follow its direction ascending steeply, passing a little wood, to the left, and a wall, with plenty of excuses for pausing to admire fine views all around. Pass just to the left of the very top of the rise, maintaining direction to reach a minor road. Turn right for about $^1/_4$ mile, passing a right turn to reach a footpath, on the left, as the road bends a little to the left. Follow this path north-north-eastwards towards Great Weeke and Yellam, descending beside a wall and hedge, to the left, to reach a narrower path at the bottom. Now continue walking north-north-eastwards to reach a gate into a wood. Continue to a junction. Here, straight on is to Great Weeke, right is to Yellam: the route turns left over a stile and heads towards Westcott Farm about $1/_3$ mile further on. Cross a stream and stile, then several more stiles and another stream to reach a farm track. Follow the track to a minor road. Turn right and after about 200 yards bear left at a junction to go past Ardley House, on the right. After a further 100 yards, leave the road along the footpath on the left. The path leads across two fields into an estate of modern houses. Continue to reach the B3206.

Turn left, with care, for a few yards, then take the footpath on the right, following it to another minor road. This crosses Rushford Bridge over the River Teign. Once over the bridge, turn left along a footpath leading along the riverbank: sometimes the path strays a little away from the river, only to return later. This section of the walk is part of the **Two Moors Way**. Follow the Way over a little footbridge and beside a weir. The route here is particularly beautiful in spring with bluebells, wood anemones and cowslips. After about a mile, Chagford Bridge is reached: turn left over the river and follow the lane back to Chagford.

POINTS OF INTEREST:

Chagford – Once a stannary (tin-mining) town and market centre, Chagford is now thriving on tourists and business from local farming. It is also a favourite with retired folk. It is said that any girl being wed from 'The Three Crowns' will meet the ghost of Mary Whiddon who, in 1641, was shot by a jealous boy-friend as she left the church with her newly-wedded husband (echoes of Lorna Doone and Dan'l Whiddon – Uncle Tom Cobley's riding companion?).

Be sure to visit the tiny public garden at the end of New Street which is famous for its wonderful views and sunsets. Chagford Bridge is 16th-century and replaced an even earlier one.

Two Moors Way – This long-distance footpath is of very recent origin, linking Exmoor and Dartmoor. It replaces a 'lost' track known as The Mariners Way which sailors used to get from Dartmouth to Bideford.

REFRESHMENTS:
The Globe Inn, Chagford.
The Bullers Arms, Chagford.
The Three Crowns, Chagford.

Walk 9   DREWSTEIGNTON AND CASTLE DROGO   5m (8km)

Maps: OS Sheets Landranger 191; Outdoor Leisure 28.

An easy walk with a wooded gorge, riverbanks and a 'stately home' halfway round. Many signposts to follow.

Start: At 736908, Drewsteignton.

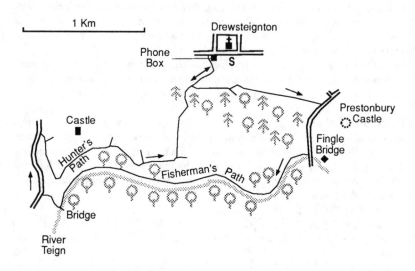

From the village of **Drewsteignton**, walk westward, passing the Drew Arms and the telephone box, and turn left, southwards, at the signpost for 'Castle Drogo'. Follow the path as it bends right, and after a further 200 yards, turn left, as signed for Fingle Bridge. After $^1/_4$ mile, at another Fingle Bridge sign, keep left and fork left again to continue to a tarmac lane. Turn right, southwards, along the lane for $^1/_3$ mile, with the Bronze-Age hill fort of Prestonbury Castle to the left, to reach granite **Fingle Bridge** itself. Pause and admire and then, perhaps after some camera-work, take the signed 'Fisherman's Path' on the near-side bank, heading upstream. This path follows the Teign for $1^1/_2$ miles: on reaching a metal footbridge, turn right to follow the signed

'Hunter's Path', ascending for 300 yards to join a driveway. Continue for another ¹/₄ mile and, at a gate and another 'Hunter's Path' sign, turn sharp right (almost a 'hairpin'!).

A visit to the **Castle Drogo** requires a short detour, to the left, as signed. To continue the walk, follow the path as it bends left, after another ¹/₄ mile (with a further path off to the left for the castle), following clear signs back to the village. Go through a gate and over a stile, then along the edges of two fields. Beyond another gate and stile, the route continues through a wooded area to reach a junction of paths. Here, continue along the signed path to reach a road. Turn right back to the start.

POINTS OF INTEREST:

Drewsteignton – This delightful, 'typically Devon' village of rectangular plan, granite and thatch cottages and the unusual inn will require extra time to explore.

Fingle Bridge – Another photogenic spot to linger. Built of granite blocks, it dates at least from the 16th century.

Castle Drogo – Built on a 900 foot hill above Teign valley, the castle was completed in 1930 to designs by Sir Edwin Lutyens for Julius Drew (who made his millions from the 'Home and Colonial' grocery store chain). An architectural 'one off' of granite with many fascinating features and excellent viewpoints, it is owned by the National Trust and open during the summer months. Croquet on the lawn is possible – you can hire the mallets etc!

REFRESHMENTS:

The Drew Arms, Drewsteignton.
The Angler's Rest, Fingle Bridge.

Walk 10 PETER AND MARY TAVY 5m (8km)

Maps: OS Sheets Landranger 191; Outdoor Leisure 28.
A fairly easy walk, some roads and, maybe, muddy tracks.
Start: At 514776, the Post Office, Peter Tavy.

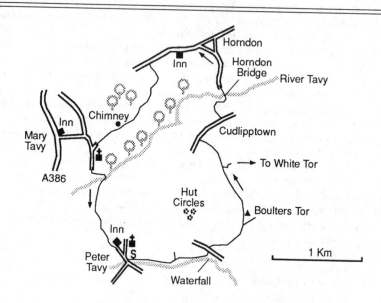

From the Post Office in the little village of **Peter Tavy** – off the A386, 3 miles north of Tavistock – walk southwards and, at the crossroads, bear left on to the bridleway signed 'Coombe'. Go left over the bridge and climb westwards, passing Combe Cottages. As the lane becomes a path and goes through a gate, keep to the 'Lower Godsworthy' path, climbing to a wall. Go over this into a field under Smeardon Down and maintain your eastward course across another field to reach another wall. Go through a gate and along a grassy path which becomes a lane. Turn left along the lane and, on reaching the signpost 'Stephen's Grave, White Tor' follow its direction (northwards) to Boulters Tor. Keep left along the grass path which runs between a wall, to the right and a row of stones, to the left. Now descend, go through a gate into a field and go over a bridge crossing a little stream to join a lane. Here keep left, still heading northwards, and walk into the hamlet of Cudlipptown. At the junction, turn right and after 350 yards follow the signed path on the left (northwards). Descend to the River Tavy, and bear right to cross it at Horndon Bridge.

Once over the bridge, follow the track northwards to arrive in Horndon. Keep left at the fork, and soon turn left (south-westwards) towards **Mary Tavy**. The **Elephant's Nest Inn** is soon reached. After a further $^1/_4$ mile, take the track on the left and follow it through fields, keeping right through two fields, then half-left through another field to reach a stone stile in a wall. Cross this and maintain the generally south-west direction, descending to the remains of an old mine working, a chimney marking the way. Follow the path over a tall stile, and at the bottom of the next field turn left. Now go through a gate on the right, heading for the church tower ahead. Go into the churchyard over a stone stile, and then swing southwards, through a gate. Go along a lane, then bear left and cross a bridge (over the Tavy again). Now follow the signed bridleway, ascending to Peter Tavy and the inn and post office where the walk began.

POINTS OF INTEREST:

Peter Tavy – This delightful Devon village has early 17th-century buildings and a church dating back to c1500.

Mary Tavy – Lead, tin and copper were all mined in the village's vicinity. Wheal Betsy engine house is a mile to the north on the A386. In the village churchyard is the grave of one William Crossing who wrote a splendid book on Dartmoor, its paths, old customs and geographical features, in the early part of the 20th century.

The twin villages grew out of settlements either side of the Tavy River. Each has a church dedicated, of course, to St Mary and St Peter.

Elephant's Nest Inn – This hostelry is marked on the OS map as 'New Inn' and was once, so the story goes, owned by a landlord of elephantine proportions. It now houses many elephant ornaments.

REFRESHMENTS:

The Peter Tavy Inn, Peter Tavy.
The Elephant's Nest, Horndon.

Walk 11   **HALLSANDS**   5m (8km)

Maps: OS Sheets Landranger 202; Outdoor Leisure 20.

Superb cliff walk and a visit to a lost village. Quiet lanes.

Start: At 821375, the Start Point car park.

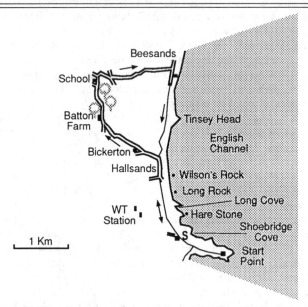

Another superb cliff walk in South Devon, plus an inland stroll along quiet lanes and a visit to a derelict fishing village. The 5 miles might seem longer – the cliff walk has its ups and downs and Hallsands is a place to linger.

From the car park, walk north along the cliff walk (part of the South Devon Coastal Path) with wireless masts up to the left, and the rocks, reefs and coves below and right. Ignore the left turn towards Hollowcombe at Wilson's Rock, continuing to the road at **Hallsands**.

After using the camera, keep ahead for a further 100 yards, then turn inland, left, on a road past a telephone kiosk. After another 200 yards, turn right and follow the road for $\frac{1}{4}$ mile to reach a left-hand bend. Follow this around, then very soon turn right along a lane to Batton Farm. Follow the lane northwards for another $\frac{1}{2}$ mile, passing the farm, to reach a road fork by a school. Keep ahead, but, after another 250 yards turn right, towards the sea. At the next lane junction, go right and soon bear left to maintain the eastward direction, reaching the coast at Beesands.

Turn right along the Coastal Path, pass the Beesands Inn and continue south for $1^1/_4$ superb miles to return to Hallsands – and another chance for the camera. Now retrace the outward journey back to the car park above Shoelodge Reef.

POINTS OF INTEREST:
Hallsands – A hundred years ago there was a flourishing village here – 20 cottages and a pub. In 1917, as part of off-shore dredging operations for shingle to assist in the building of Devonport, the beach was left so unprotected that the winter gales wrought havoc and the population of fishermen and their families were forced to leave.

REFRESHMENTS:
The Beesands Inn, Beesands.

Walk 12   **DALWOOD AND HEATHSTOCK**   5m (8km)

Maps: OS Sheets Landranger 192; Pathfinder 1297.

Quiet country lanes and bridleways – can be muddy and there are some steep bits.

Start: At 248004, the Tucker's Arms, Dalwood.

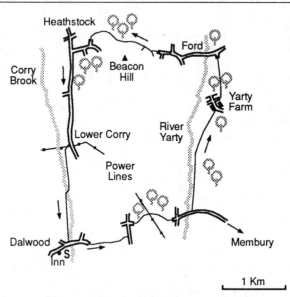

Leave the Tuckers Arms Inn in **Dalwood** – which lies off the A35, 10 miles east of Honiton – turning right along the road to cross the river. Now leave the road by keeping ahead along a farm access road just to the right of the telephone box. Go through a gate and maintain the east-north-easterly direction across fields, going uphill to reach a drive just to the right of a house. Follow this to emerge on to a lane. Turn left to reach a junction. Turn right and follow a lane until it ends at a grass track just past a house. Go through the gate on the left and walk down the field beyond to reach a signpost and stile. Go over and continue descending to reach a gate. Go through and bear left along a lane. Now keep ahead on the Membury road to cross the bridge over the River Yarty.

A few yards further on, turn left through a gate and head due north, following the river on a clear track for almost a mile. Eventually the track climbs away from the river towards Yarty Farm, leading to a gate and the access lane to the farm. Do not turn left nor go straight into the farmhouse buildings: instead, go right, through a little wood and at the top keep straight ahead, going through a gate and then along a gravel track leading down to a ford across the River Yarty. If the ford is too deep, there are two bridges through the hedge on the left. Continue along the track to reach a lane. Turn right and bear left at the next junction. Now at a fork, bear right along a bridleway, heading westwards and ascending towards Beacon Hill. Bear right near the top, then go downhill as the track widens. Go between houses and continue, to emerge on to a lane in the hamlet of Heathstock.

Turn right and follow the lane to a T-junction. Turn left, southwards, along an attractive lane, following it for almost $1\frac{1}{2}$ miles to reach Lower Corry. Here, turn right through a gate opposite a house on the left (and before reaching the power cables). Now go left behind a farm, and descend to Corry Brook. Bear left and keep alongside the Brook, without crossing it, for $\frac{1}{4}$ mile, then cross by way of a wooden bridge to reach the west bank. Turn right to continue southwards. Go through a gate on to a lane and turn right back to The Tucker's Arms.

POINTS OF INTEREST:
Dalwood – Set between Axminster and Honiton, just off the A35, this is an attractive little village (that was once in Dorset!), and the centre of many Devonshire farms. At one time tanning, weaving and soap making were important local industries, with mills grinding flour, milling malt and making woollen cloth. There is a delightful little church – St Peter's – dating from the early 15th century and a Baptist Chapel, with records going back to 1653, that has been re-thatched and restored with deal box pews and, below the floorboards, a baptistery for total immersion! On the edge of the village is Telegraph Cottage: there used to be a semaphore station here when messages were sent by that method from Plymouth to London during Napoleonic times.

REFRESHMENTS:
The Tucker's Arms, Dalwood. The inn dates back to the 13th century – but the food and drinks are fresh!

Walk 13   MORTEHOE AND LEE   5m (8km)

Maps: OS Sheets Landranger 180; Pathfinder 1213.
Quiet farmland, coastal path and two North Devon villages.
Start: At 456452, the Ship Aground Inn, Mortehoe.

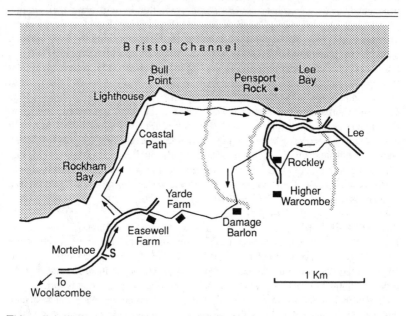

This walk is likely to take a bit longer as it is full of places to rest and linger – especially on a warm summer's day.

From the Ship Aground in **Mortehoe**, follow the road north-eastwards for 500 yards (as signed 'for Lighthouse and Lee') and then go left down a lane (signed 'for Rockham Beach'). Go through a gate and follow the footpath beyond along the valley, heading northwards, to join the South West Coastal Path at a stile. Now follow the Path to reach the beach at Rockham, where there is a paddling opportunity! Ascend northwards and then north-eastwards along the cliffs – this section is up and down, and can be demanding in hot weather – for $^3/_4$ mile to reach the **lighthouse** at Bull Point. Descend steps, then go up to the gates, cross the road walk alongside the wall. Continue eastwards, with more ups and downs, crossing two streams and enjoying views northwards to Wales. After almost a mile, join a road which descends into **Lee**.

28

Turn right along a path signed 'Lee and Toilets', then walk beside a car park. Now follow a wire fence until it turns right. Here, go through a gate and walk along a wall to reach another gate. Go through and continue over a little brook and along a path signed 'Hr Warcombe'. This path leads up through woodland and across an access track, right, to reach a stile. Cross and bear right to emerge on to open ground. Now bear left around the hill top, then go over a field towards Rockley. Keeping this on your right, cross another stile on to a road. Turn right and follow the road for a short $\frac{1}{4}$ mile, then turn left over another stile. Follow the field track beyond to reach a farm track. After a further $\frac{1}{4}$ mile, keep left and follow the clear right-of-way sign through **Damage Barton**, passing in front of the farmhouse and climbing westwards along a lane. Next, follow the sign 'Footpath to Mortehoe', going alongside a hedge to the right. Cross two fields and a stile, and then go half-left to reach a field corner. Go through the gate on the right and follow further 'Mortehoe' signs through Easewell Farm and a caravan site. At the main gate, turn left and follow the road back to the village and the start.

POINTS OF INTEREST:

Mortehoe – In days past the main industries hereabouts were wreck-salvage and smuggling. Thankfully, farming and tourism have replaced them. The village church, dedicated to St Mary, has Norman doors, a 13th-century tower and good bench-ends.
Lighthouse – The new lighthouse at Bull Point was completed in 1975 and warns shipping of a very inhospitable coastline.
Lee – This very picturesque village has many delightful cottages, an inn and an early Victorian church built in Neo-gothic style.
Damage Barton – Damage Barton Farm has a Tudor farmhouse, walled gardens and a byre of shale that looks like piles of coins.

REFRESHMENTS:
The Grampus, Lee.
The Ship Aground, Mortehoe.
There are also other possibilities in Mortehoe, and a good range of opportunities can be found at Woolacoombe, 2 miles south of Mortehoe.

Walk 14   BRANSCOMBE AND BEER   5m (8km)

Maps: OS Sheets Landranger 192; Pathfinder 1316.

A short, but demanding, walk - cliffs 'ups and downs', stiles and open common.

Start: At 207881, the car park at Branscombe Mouth.

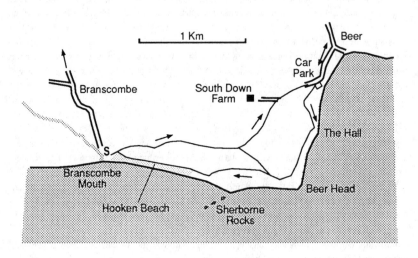

From the car park at Branscombe Mouth, which lies south of the A3052, the Sidmouth to Seaton road, walk eastwards towards Hooken Beach. Soon, at a four-way sign (follow 'Hooken Cliffs and Beer') strike steeply uphill to reach a gate. Go through and up the steps beyond. Climb a stile and, at the top, veer half-right to follow the cliff-edge fence to a Coastguard Lookout point. Here, go half-left, following the path signed 'Public Footpath', not the one signed to 'Beer'. This path leads away from the Coastal Path to join a farm track. Go through a gate, across a cattle grid and descend along a farm access lane to reach a junction in **Beer**.

A short detour to the left at the lane junction will take the walker to refreshments and the main village of Beer, but the walk continues by heading westward from the cliff-top car park, following the signed path for 'Branscombe Mouth 1³/₄m'. Descend stone steps and turn right, then, by the caravan park, turn left at another cliff path sign. The route is now clearly marked by the yellow footpath and acorn signs of the **South West Coastal Path**, heading due south for a short mile to reach another Coastguard Lookout at Beer Head. On a good day, the views from here are splendid: Beer and Seaton Bay lie to the left (east), with Weymouth far off; while to the right are Hooken Beach, Branscombe, Sidmouth and Budleigh Salterton.

On arriving at another signpost, keep left and cross a stile. Now descend behind Sherborne Rocks to reach a track which runs alongside the beach. Follow the rough concrete path, passing caravans before arriving at Branscombe Mouth and the start.

POINTS OF INTEREST:

Beer – Beer has been a popular seaside place since prehistoric times as flints were worked and traded from Beer Head in those days! The Romans also used local stone, quarrying it and using the sheltered cove at Beer to export it by boat. While in the town, be sure to visit the Lace Shop where Queen Victoria's wedding dress was made – the village was once a famous lace-making centre, the trade started by Flemish craftsmen and women who settled here in the latter half of the 16th century. Herring fishing was also very important in the past - as were smuggling and supplying sailors for the Royal Navy. Nowadays it is mostly mackerel fishing and tourists – sometimes both together.

The South West Coastal Path – The Path was officially 'completed' and opened in 1978. It runs from Minehead in Somerset via Lands End to a point near Poole in Dorset, covering 567 miles of cliff-top, sand, shingle, pebble, old railway, grassy common, riverbank, farm track and pavement. Much of it is strenuous walking, with hundreds of ups and downs to test the keenest walker, and some parts are subject to erosion and subsidence so care must be taken and temporary warning notices heeded. Wild flowers, prehistoric sites, clean and bracing air and bird songs are just some of the outstanding features.

REFRESHMENTS:

A good selection can be found at Beer, conveniently positioned halfway round the walk.

Walk 15   **POWDERHAM AND EXMINSTER**   5m (8km)

Maps: OS Sheets Landranger 192; Pathfinder 1329.

A bird-watching walk on the Exe estuary. Flat, easy and quiet.

Start: At 967842, in Powderham.

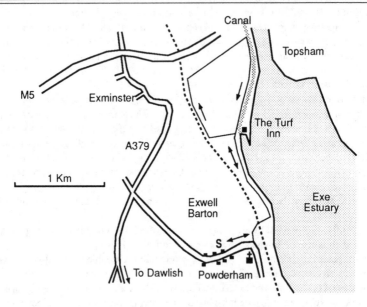

From Powderham, which lies on a minor road off the A379 about 8 miles north of Dawlish, walk eastwards to the **Church of St Clements** and, as the road bends to the right, go through the gate on the left, and walk alongside the railway line. After about 200 yards, at a gate, cross the line, with great care, and turn left alongside the river - at the confluence of the rivers Exe and Clyst. Now walk northwards and then north-westwards for almost a mile, following the river to reach The Turf Inn.

Opposite the inn, climb the high stile to follow a footpath, on the left, away from the estuary, going across fields towards the railway line once more. On reaching the line, do not cross: instead, turn right and walk for a further $^1/_2$ mile to reach a lane at a bridge on the outskirts of Exminster. (A detour left here, over the bridge, leads to **Exminster** where refreshments are readily available.) The route does not cross the bridge, turning right along the lane and heading back towards the river.

Before reaching the river, cross a drainage ditch and then take the signed footpath half-left to reach the **Exeter Canal** which runs parallel to the river bank. Turn right along the towpath for about $1\frac{1}{4}$ miles to reach the Turf Inn again. Now cross the lock in front of the pub and so regain the footpath which was used on the outward journey. Now reverse the outward journey, once again enjoying the views across the **estuary** and remembering to take great care when re-crossing the railway line.

POINTS OF INTEREST:

St Clement's Church, Powderham – The church is listed as an historical and architectural building of outstanding merit. It is built of Old Red Sandstone brick, has a font dating from 1258 and very ancient timber doors.

Exminster – There is an old church here too, parts dating back to the 13th century. The original village has been developed this century and now has many modern residences, though the inn makes a detour worthwhile.

Exeter Canal – This is considered to be the oldest canal in Britain having been in use since 1566.

Estuary – Because the muddy estuary is rich in molluscs, worms, etc. it is a very attractive place for birds. Flocks of dunlin, merganser, curlew and whimbrel are common. The rarer avocet can sometimes be seen, while gulls, terns and cormorants are everywhere.

In summer there are many species of butterfly to be spotted, as well as damselflies and dragonflies galore.

REFRESHMENTS:

The Turf Inn, on the route.

There are other possibilities if the detour to Exminster is taken.

Walk 16   IPPLEPEN AND BROADHEMPSTON   5¹/₂m (9km)

Maps: OS Sheets Landranger 202; Pathfinder 1351.

A gentle walk through quiet Devon countryside and villages.

Start: At 834665, Ipplepen Church.

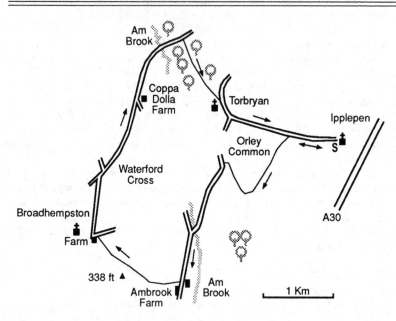

Begin at the church in **Ipplepen,** which lies jut off the A381, halfway between Newton Abbott and Totnes. Walk westwards along a road signposted for Broadhempston, but in a short ¹/₂ mile turn left through a gate on to a track leading on to the edge of the very attractive Orley Common. In season, the Common has a wide range of wild flowers, which should be enjoyed but not picked. Now head south for about ¹/₃ mile, then go sharp right for another ¹/₃ mile to reach a junction of lanes at the south-west corner of the Common. Follow the lane to the left, going downhill and crossing a bridge over the Am Brook. Very soon after, go left, southwards, following a road for ³/₄ mile to reach Ambrook Farm.

Turn right beside the farmhouse and cross a field, heading due west, to reach a gate in the far right corner. Go through and, keeping the hedge and fence on your left, head north-westwards, uphill, to reach a stile. Cross and maintain direction, enjoying the distant views of Dartmoor. Cross further stiles and go through gates – the way is well marked – then keep to the left of a hedge as it goes gently downhill to reach a right-hand field corner. Here, follow a stony track which leads down to farm buildings. The track continues to the outskirts of the village of Broadhempston. Keep down the hill (go left for the inn) and then go up Church Hill, heading northwards and passing Hembury Cottages to reach Waterford Cross, about $^1/_4$ mile out of the village. Here, bear right along a lane, following it all the way to Coppa Dolla Farm. Go past the farm and descend to cross Am Brook again. Now go uphill, passing an old quarry, to the left, and a private access road.

Now cross a stone slab stile to the right and follow the path beyond eastwards, making for woodland. Cross another stile into the woodland and follow the clear path through it to reach a drive. Bear left and go through the Old Rectory gardens. Go through a gate and along the bottom of several fields, with the lime-washed tower of Torbryan's church off to the right, to reach an iron gate on to a lane. Go right, and right again into **Torbryan**. For refreshments, go up the 'No Through Road', to the right, to reach the village inn.

The route continues by going straight on, not towards the inn. Where the lane swings right, keep left to go along the north edge of Orley Common, passing the gate, on the right, used to reach the Common earlier on the walk. Continue along the road, reversing the outward route back to Ipplepen and the start.

POINTS OF INTEREST:

Ipplepen – Now a dormitory for Totnes and Newton Abbott, this village was once a farming and quarrying – for limestone and marble – centre. St Andrew's Church is a tranquil spot on a warm summer's day. In the latter half of the last century Arthur Conan Doyle was a regular visitor to a friend in the village and *The Hound of the Baskervilles* was conceived here.

Torbryan – Trinity Church, with its starkly white tower, has a very interesting interior too – paintings of forty saints and enclosed pews are but two special features.

REFRESHMENTS:

The Monk's Retreat, Broadhempston.
The Church House Inn, Torbryan.
There are possibilities in Ipplepen.

Walk 17 HANGER DOWN AND ERME RIVER 5½m (9km)

Maps: OS Sheets Landranger 202; Outdoor Leisure 28.

An easy, but possibly muddy, walk around the moor and along the river bank.

Start: At 636562, the car park in Ivybridge.

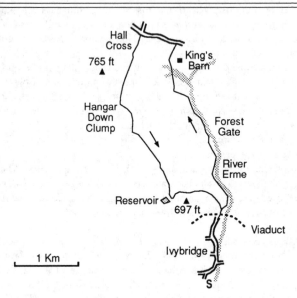

Ensuring suitable footwear for muddy conditions after rain, walk north from the car park in **Ivybridge** towards the railway viaduct. Leave the road along the track to the right, going down to the bank of the River Erme. Turn left, heading northwards to go under the railway line. Go past a concrete basin, to the left, and through pines and deciduous trees to reach a ladder stile at Forest Gate. Continue along the river – waymarks assisting – for a long 1¼ mile from the viaduct. Sometimes the track leaves the water's edge, but often it is virtually on the water and stepping-stones are necessary!. Eventually, the track bears clearly left, crosses a little stream and follows a fence to reach a gate. Go through and down across the hill. Now go up into conifers and continue ahead to emerge into a field. Here, turn right, through a gap, into a second field, with King's Barn off to the right. Soon an old drover's road, now a bridleway, is reached: follow it across a stream and on to a lane.

Turn left along the lane for $1/_2$ mile to reach a junction at Hall Cross. Turn left, southwards, going through beeches to reach open moor. Maintain the southerly direction, heading for Hanger Down Clump, the trees about $3/_4$ mile ahead. About 200 yards before reaching the Clump, swing off to the left, going around the trees and then heading southwards again, towards a square-topped mound (a reservoir) about $3/_4$ mile distant. At the reservoir's fence, keep left to the corner and continue southwards again, going between enclosure fences and on to reach a gate. Go through on to Henlake Down. Turn left, due east, following a path as it descends towards a large house in the distance, gently at first then much steeper. After a further $1/_4$ mile, as the path forks, keep left and go down to a lane. Turn right to return to the viaduct and retrace the road back to the start in Ivybridge.

POINTS OF INTEREST:

Ivybridge – Ivybridge was once just a little village, but local water-power from the fast-flowing Erme enabled a thriving paper-making industry to develop, employing many people and expanding the village in to a town. The nearby farms still produce milk and meat as they have done for many centuries.

REFRESHMENTS:

Nothing on the route, but Ivybridge has a wide variety of cafés, restaurants and inns.

Walk 18   HUNTER'S INN AND TRENTISHOE   5$\frac{1}{2}$m (9km)

Maps: OS Sheets Landranger 180; Pathfinder 1214.

A varied and easy walk with woods, dramatic scenery and a pleasant beach.

Start: At 654480, Hunter's Inn.

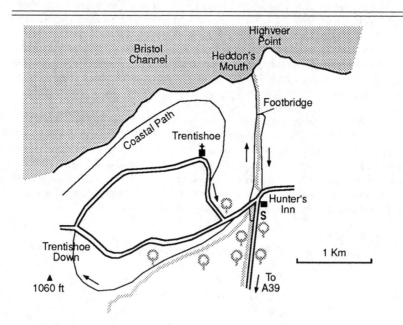

This popular short walk may well take a long time to complete as it has many splendid viewpoints at which to linger, as well as an inviting beach to laze on and paddle from.

Leaving the car park at the Hunter's Inn, turn left to pass the Inn. Go across two bridges and take a road off to the right, then turn left down the lane signed to 'Trentishoe Mill'. Soon, bear left off the lane on to a path which follows the stream and goes into the trees. Follow this path for a splendid mile, eventually ascending to reach a fork. Take the left branch out on to the Trentishoe Down.

Bear right, contouring around the Down, pausing to admire the views inland before soon descending to reach a road. Cross and follow the minor road opposite to reach the hamlet and church at **Trentishoe**. From the church, continue down the lane to reach a T-junction. Turn left, but after 30 yards, and before crossing a bridge, turn left through a gate to follow a track signed for 'Heddon's Mouth'.

With the little River Heddon to the right, follow the track down towards the sea, passing a little bridge, to the right, and a ruined **lime kiln** before descending to the beach. The walk is completed by returning to the bridge, crossing it and following the stream on the other bank, ascending for $^3/_4$ mile to return to the **Hunter's Inn** and car park.

POINTS OF INTEREST:
Trentishoe – Spare time to explore the tiny church with its quaint little musician's gallery which has a space cut out of the balcony so that the bass viol player could move his arm freely.
Lime kiln – The kiln near the beach is a reminder of the times when lime was brought across from South Wales, together with coal, and burnt here to convert it to a 'sweetener' for spreading on the local acid soil. The coasters took pit props back for use in the coal mines.
Hunter's Inn – There's been an inn here for more than 1250 years. The inn was once a thatched cottage, but this burnt down in 1895 to be replaced by the present Swiss-chalet-style building.

REFRESHMENTS:
The Hunter's Inn, at the start of the walk.

BLACKAWTON

$5^1/_2$m (9km)

Maps: OS Sheets Landranger 202; Outdoor Leisure 20.
South Devon footpaths and country lanes.
Start: At 805510, Blackawton Church.

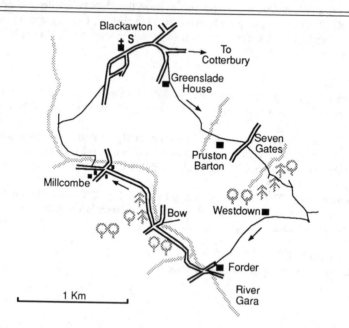

Situated in the South Hams district of South Devon the lovely village of **Blackawton** should be explored before or after the walk, which commences from St Michael's Church.

Take the road to Cotterbury, but soon fork right. Now continue along the road for 100 yards, then bear left along a, usually muddy, lane by Greenslade House. After crossing a little stream, maintain the south-easterly direction to pass to the rear of Pruston Barton Farm. Now ascend to reach a road at Seven Gates. Go straight over, still heading south-eastwards, with an iron barn to the left, and go downhill towards a stream and woodland. Cross the stream, go through a gate and continue uphill. Ignore a track to the right, but go right at a signed post, still ascending and going through trees after a $^1/_4$ mile.

The direction is now westwards and south-westwards, passing Westdown Farm, to the right, and then going along a lane, downhill, to reach Forder. Cross the Gara River and bear right, north-westwards, keeping the river on your right. Continue straight on at the two next crossroads (Bow and Millcombe). Then , about 120 yards beyond Millcombe House, take the signed footpath on the right. Follow the path to a narrow footbridge. Cross and continue to reach a lane.

Turn left, heading due west, to reach a house. Keep behind the buildings to the right, following the waymarkers to reach some steps. Descend, go over a stile and cross a stream by stepping-stones to reach a field. Continue along the field edge to reach the far right corner where there is a gate and a 'no through' sign. Take the path to the right, going through bushes to reach another gate and, again, some steps and stile. Go up the steps to enter a field. Now ascend steeply, with a hedge on your left, and then follow more waymarkers to reach a road. Turn right, then left to return to the church.

POINTS OF INTEREST:

Blackawton – Although it is 4 miles inland, the sea is in view from this delightful village, which was certainly settled in Saxon times. The church boasts a large Norman font and a fine rood screen. Sir Walter Raleigh is reputed to have wed Elizabeth Throckmorton here. A church charity, dating back to 1699, provides free bread to poor parishioners every Sunday. Nowadays it is given to local children who clamour for the dry bread!

Vines are grown locally and there is also a brewery in the village. Blackawton was totally evacuated during part of World War II so that US forces could prepare for the Normandy invasion, as was much of the South Hams district, and nearby Sheplegh Court became Eisenhower's headquarters for a time.

REFRESHMENTS:
The George Inn, Blackawton.
The Normandy Arms, Blackawton.

Walk 20   **IDDESLEIGH AND UPCOTT**   5$\frac{1}{2}$m (9km)

Maps: OS Sheets Landranger 191; Pathfinder 1293.

Easy walk through quiet Devon farmland and lanes, part of the Tarka Trail.

Start: At 570083, the Duke of York Inn, Iddesleigh.

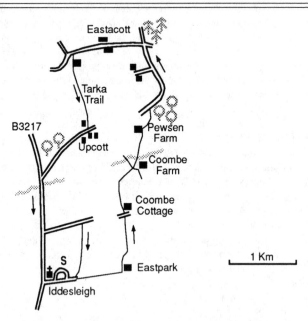

From the inn at **Iddesleigh**, go eastward along a gravel track for a short $\frac{1}{2}$ mile to reach the farm buildings of Eastpark. There, follow the track around to the left, go through a gate and continue for another $\frac{1}{2}$ mile to reach a lane. Cross straight over and maintain direction along a track, passing Coombe Cottage, to the right. Follow the track to Coombe Farm. Go through a wooden gate on the left, and then keep right (north-eastwards) to cross a stream. Now follow a track northwards, passing Pewsen Farm, just to the left. Follow the farm's access lane for 250 yards to reach a lane. Turn right and follow the lane as it bends left. Ignore another access lane, to the left, continuing to reach a junction of lanes by a clump of conifer trees.

Turn left and follow a lane for about $^3/_4$ mile, passing Eastacott, to reach a T-junction. Just before this junction, turn left along the access lane to another farm. Go downhill, cross a stream and then go uphill to reach a lane and the hamlet of Uppacott, following a section of the **Tarka Trail**. Turn right along the lane, going downhill and admiring the views across the valley of the river Torridge. At the bottom, turn left, with care, along the main B3217. Walk uphill to the Baptist Church, then turn left, along a lane signed 'Whitemore and Hennacroft'. The lane goes uphill, but you shortly take a public footpath on the right, going across a field to reach an iron gate. Go through and walk down to a second gate. Go through on to a track and turn right to return to Iddesleigh.

POINTS OF INTEREST:

Iddesleigh – The cob and thatch cottages around a village green are 'typical Devon'. The 15th-century church is dedicated to St James and once had a curate named Jack Russell who bred the terrier that now carries his name.

Tarka Trail – Henry Williamson's classic book *Tarka the Otter* gives the theme to a trail which takes walkers through countryside between Dartmoor and Exmoor, along streams and past small settlements little changed since the 1920s. For further information contact the Tarka Country Tourist Association, PO Box 4, Chulmleigh, EX18 7YX (01837-83399). The Tarka Gallery in the North Devon Museum, at The Square, Barnstaple, is well worth a visit.

REFRESHMENTS:
Duke of York, Iddesleigh.

Walk 21   BUCKLAND-IN-THE-MOOR   6m (9½km)

Maps: OS Sheets Landranger 191; Outdoor Leisure 28.

An easy walk – little woods, little lanes and little brooks.

Start: At 721732, the church, Buckland-in-the Moor.

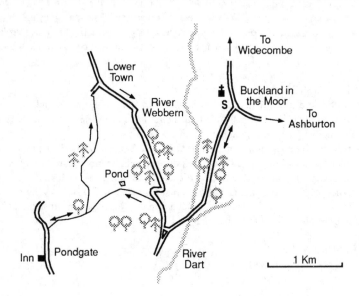

The walk starts at the church in **Buckland-in-the Moor**, on the Widecombe road north-west of Ashburton.

Leave the church by walking south (towards Ashburton) along the road for a few yards to reach a fork. Take the right branch, heading south-westwards downhill along a quiet lane and into woodland. Follow the lane for a mile to reach Buckland Bridge, where the Dart meets the Webburn. Cross the bridge and continue along the lane for a further ¼ mile to reach a junction with a grassy triangle. Turn right, and then sharp right to follow a lane northwards. At the next sharp right bend, leave the lane to the left, following a bridleway that heads north-west through conifers and mixed woodland.

After ¹/₂ mile, keep to the left of a pond and then go along the right edge of three fields, using gates and stiles to pass between them, to reach the lane – often fairly busy! – just north of Poundsgate. On this section of the walk to the lane, you will pass a signpost for 'Lower Town' – note this as you will be returning to this point. To reach refreshments when the lane is joined, turn left into the hamlet of Poundsgate for the welcome sight of the Tavistock Inn.

Retrace your steps from the Inn, but turn left at the signpost for 'Lower Town' which was passed earlier. Those not making the detour to the Tavistock Inn will turn right here. Go round a field to reach a gate, to the right, on to a drive. Bear left by some houses and obey a signpost to go up to a farm track. The route is northwards now, right and left, going through gates to emerge on to a lane at Lower Town.

Turn right and walk along the lane for a long mile to reach the grassy triangle between lanes passed on the outward journey. Turn left and retrace the outward route back to Buckland.

POINTS OF INTEREST:

In spring this walk offers spectacular displays of wild flowers along the way, and equally spectacular woodland section at the start and finish. The lane leading south-eastwards from Lower Town is particularly beautiful.

Buckland-in-the-Moor – This delightful village has a local stone built church dedicated to St Peter and containing panel paintings on rood screens and an unusual church tower clock – 'My Dear Mother' replacing the usual numerals. To the east there are some much photographed thatched cottages – chocolate box or jigsaw puzzle stuff – and on the Beacon (also to the east, but off the walk) there are stone tablets carved with The Ten Commandments.

REFRESHMENTS:

The Tavistock Inn, Poundsgate. This fine inn is more than 700 years old.
There are also a café and tea rooms in Buckland.

Walk 22   HOUND TOR AND BECKA FALLS   6m (9½km)

Maps: OS Sheets Landranger 191; Outdoor Leisure 28.

Open moorland, leafy streams, a popular waterfall and some stunning views.

Start: At 739792, Hound Tor car park.

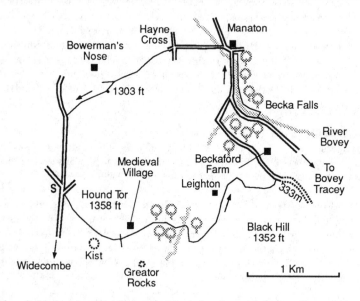

Although this is a shortish 'day' walk, it includes plenty of places to linger so it might take longer than anticipated.

Commence by walking back to the junction of minor roads 50 yards south of the car park. Continue south, towards Widecombe-in-the-Moor, for a few yards, then take the track on the left, heading south-eastwards, with Hound Tor to the left. A detour is needed to reach the Tor's top as the route goes around the southern side of the peak to reach an ancient cairn circle and kist a short ½ mile from the road. Now ignore the clear bridleway crossing north-south, going half-left and downhill, with the site of a **Medieval Village**, a few yards to the left. Go through two wall-gaps and a gate, then walk alongside a little copse, on the left, with Greator Rocks off to the right.

46

Continue along the clear track through several gates and a pair of stone posts, then cross a little stream. Continue to reach, and cross, a little clapper bridge over Becka Brook, then go up steps into a wood. Ascend, keeping to the right of more trees, then turn north-eastwards, inside walled **'new takes'**, to pass the settlement of Leighon, to the left, and the cairns on Black Hill $\frac{1}{2}$ mile off to the right. Continue along the bridleway as it contours around the higher land, heading northwards, then eastwards to reach sign for 'Upper Terrace Drive'. Go along the farm track to reach a T-junction with a minor road, near the 1093 feet (333m) spot height.

Turn left and follow the road for almost a mile, crossing Beckaford Bridge and continuing to reach a junction. Turn right to the very popular, but, as a consequence, sometimes crowded, beauty spot of Becka Falls, about $\frac{1}{3}$ mile along the busy lane to the south-east. Having lingered, and perhaps had some refreshment, cross the river and go up the steps at the base of the falls to reach a path-fork. Turn left and follow the River Bovey through woodland for $\frac{3}{4}$ mile to emerge on to the road again. Turn right to reach the Kestor Inn.

Opposite the inn, turn left along a lane signed for 'Southcot', following it to a crossroads at Hayne Cross. Go straight ahead along the lane opposite (signed for 'Hayne Down'). This tarmac lane soon becomes gravel, then earth: continue along it to reach a gate. Go through on to open moorland, following a bridleway heading south-westwards. When the track divides, take the left branch, which is still a bridleway, ascending and aiming for the triangular-pointed rock ahead (marked as a spot height of 1302 feet – 397m – on the Outdoor Leisure map). On reaching this point, note the Bowerman's Nose $\frac{1}{4}$ mile off to the right and enjoy all the other possible views before descending towards the Hound Tor car park (there are usually cars visible to mark the finishing-line). The track actually reaches the road about $\frac{1}{2}$ mile north of the car park: a left turn is therefore required to return to the start.

POINTS OF INTEREST:

Medieval Village – The foundations, fire places and ruined walls of Hundatora offer a special fascination on this fine walk. The village is now thought to have been abandoned after the Black Death of 1348. The site has been extensively excavated in recent years.

New Takes – Takes are land reclaimed from the open moor for grazing livestock or growing crops. It is usually walled but sometimes fenced.

REFRESHMENTS:

The Kestor Inn, on the route.
Ice-cream and light refreshments are also available at Becka Falls.

Maps: OS Sheets Landranger 191; Outdoor Leisure 28.

Dartmoor lanes, a lovely wooded valley and some prehistory.

Start: At 534724, Sampford Spiney Church.

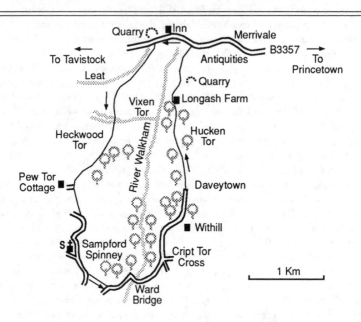

By starting at the little hamlet of **Sampford Spiney** this walk can be broken by a welcome stop at **Merrivale**, about halfway round, for refreshments and a visit to the nearby 'antiquities'. Sampford Spiney is located on a minor road 4 miles north-east of Horrabridge, off the A386. Considerate parking will be necessary in the narrow lanes.

From the church, walk south for about 250 yards to reach a junction of lanes. Go left for 300 yards, heading south-westwards to reach another junction at 'Stoneycroft'. Here, keep straight on along a sunken track, descending steeply to reach the track's junction with a lane, near a cattle grid. Turn left, following the lane into woodland. Continue along the lane as it swings right and crosses the River Walkham over Ward Bridge. Beyond, the lane ascends steeply to Cript Tor Cross, At this crossroads, turn left along the lane signed to Daveytown. There now follows a splendid walk along a mile of Devon lane, heading northwards to the hamlet of Daveytown. There, another signpost indicates 'Merrivale $1^1/_2$'. Follow this stony bridlepath through gates, passing Hucken Tor, to the right, and disused quarries to reach a bridge over a little stream. Cross and continue to another bridge. Cross this to reach Longash Farm, with Vixen Tor off to the left. Go through the farmyard and continue along the bridleway to reach the main B3357 road.

To visit the site of many ancient settlements and hut circles, turn right, with care, for $^3/_4$ mile. The route continues by turning left, also with care, to reach The Dartmoor Inn.

From the inn, continue uphill along the road, again with care, for a $^1/_4$ mile, then turn left opposite a quarry entrance to reach the open moor, heading south-westwards. At first the way is alongside a **leat**, to the right, and a stone wall, to the left, but you maintain the direction as the leat swings away to the right. Soon the rocky summit of Vixen Tor is seen ahead and the walk heads still south-westwards, and then south, away from both the wall and the Tor. Cross several small brooks, (the going here is sometimes boggy, with stepping stones assisting a dry passage), beyond which the track becomes rather faint. As long as the south-westwards course is maintained, there will be no problem: so continue uphill with a wall well off to the left and the rocky landscape of Heckwood Tor just off to the right. Soon, the debris of a granite quarry is seen to the left and the church at Sampford Spiney comes into view ahead. The track now winds southwards to join the gravel access drive of Pew Tor Cottage, to the right. Continue for a further $^1/_4$ mile to meet a lane. Continue ahead, south-eastwards, along the lane for 100 yards, then bear right with the lane to return to the church.

POINTS OF INTEREST:
Sampford Spiney – The village is little more than a collection of scattered farms and houses, with no shop, pub or post office. But it does have a delightful little church built on 14th-century foundations and room for only six at a time at the altar rail for communion.

Merrivale – This area was obviously an important place in Bronze Age times, with so many remains of settlements, rows and circles.

Leats – There are many leats on the moors, man-made mini-canals to take water down to farms and mines. They are wonderfully constructed to follow the land's contours and so provide a gentle downhill flow.

REFRESHMENTS:
The Dartmoor Inn, Merrivale. The inn was originally a collection of stone-quarrymen's houses and stands at about 1000 feet above sea level.

Walk 24 **SHIPLEY BRIDGE AND SOUTH BRENT** 6m (9$\frac{1}{2}$km)

Maps: OS Sheets Landranger 202; Outdoor Leisure 28.

An easy walk contrasting leafy lanes, a river valley and some open moorland.

Start: At 681630, the car park at Shipley Bridge.

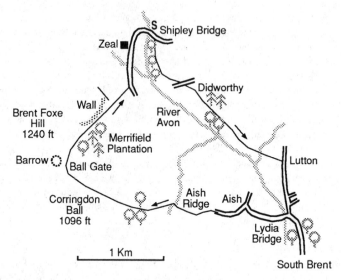

From Shipley Bridge car park, which lies to the north of South Brent, walk along the lane running southwards, with the River Avon on your right. As the lane turns left, follow the footpath signed 'Lutton via Didworthy', via a gate and stile, bearing left beyond these to reach a second stile. Cross and continue through a little wood to reach and cross two more stiles. Now go through another gate and cross directly over a lane to reach Didworthy. The way ahead is clear, going along the River Avon valley with a wood, to the right. Go past houses and through gates, following paths edged with trees and hedges, and descending to reach a ford, about 1$\frac{1}{2}$ miles from Didworthy. Beyond, go uphill into Lutton. On reaching a lane-junction, turn right, heading due south, for a long $^1/_2$ mile to reach Lydia Bridge. The walk turns right over the bridge, but for refreshments go straight on into the little market town of **South Brent**, following the footpath along the riverbank.

From Lydia Bridge, the walk follows the lane for $^1/_4$ mile to reach the hamlet of Aish. Here, as the lane turns right, take a track by the post-box, to the left, following it past Gribblesdown to reach Aish Ridge. Here there is a bridleway sign by a gate: bear left to cross the open ridge for a short $^1/_2$ mile, then go right along an enclosed path, going through gates and gently ascending to Ball Gate. Turn right, north-eastwards, along the bridleway signed to 'Shipley Bridge via Diamond Lane', with an enclosure-wall to the right and a clump of trees (Merrifield Plantation) ahead. Leave the wall as it turns off to the right, walking alongside the trees as the wall returns. Maintain direction for a mile, the path becoming a rocky track. Go through a gate, descending to pass Zeal, then follow a lane across a cattle grid and continue back to **Shipley Bridge**.

POINTS OF INTEREST:

South Brent – The town gets its name from 'brant' meaning 'steep' - Brent Hill being the rise ahead as the walk approaches Lutton.

Shipley Bridge – The ruins of a naptha-extraction plant can be found to the west of the bridge as well as china-clay ponds and old rail-trackways.

REFRESHMENTS:

There is a good selection of inns and cafes in South Brent.

Walk 25   **ROUND BURRATOR RESERVOIR**   6m (9¹/₂km)

Maps: OS Sheets Landranger 201 and 202; Outdoor Leisure 28.

A level walk (apart from one good climb), footpaths and lanes on Dartmoor.

Start: At 568694, the car park at Norsworthy Bridge.

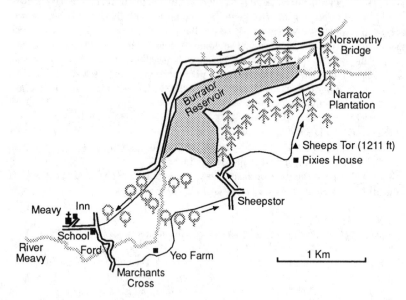

Choose a clear day and, en route, keep looking back to make the most of the splendid views. And do remember to take your camera.

From the car park walk westward along the road which runs along the northern shore of **Burrator Reservoir**. Although this road is not right at the water's edge there are many glimpses of the 'lake' through the pine forest. After about 1¹/₄ miles the road turns left (south) and runs closer to the shore, passing a pretty waterfall before arriving at the dam at the reservoir's south-west end. Here, leave the road as it turns off right and walk a little left to descend into deciduous woodland, with a gorge below and left. This path emerges into pasture after about ¹/₂ mile, then crosses a lane and goes back into woodland. Further on again, another lane, at the edge of **Meavy** village, is reached. The walk turns left, here but Meavy is well worth a short detour, to visit the village green, the church and to take the opportunity for rest and refreshments, so first take the lane ahead, with the school to the left and after a short $^1/_4$ mile turn right to reach The Royal Oak.

Returning to the school at the lane junction, turn right and descend to a ford. Use the stepping-stones, or the bridge, continuing along the lane to reach Marchants Cross (with boundary and trackway marker). Turn left and continue eastward along the lane to Yeo Farm. Just short of the buildings, turn right along a clear track which soon bears left to join another track. Now walk north along the edge of Burrator Wood. The path enters the wood and turns right, but soon emerges from the trees and continues along three field edges. Go diagonally across the fourth field to reach a lane. Turn left and follow the lane into the village of **Sheepstor**.

At a lane junction, with the church off to the right, turn left and then go first right. After 200 yards, as the lane bends round to the left towards the reservoir, take the bridleway on the right. Soon, go through a gate on to the open moor and strike directly ahead to the top of Sheeps Tor (1,211 feet – 369m), a fairly stiff, but very rewarding, climb for the extensive views from the summit. To descend, walk northwards, heading for the right-hand end of the reservoir. Aim for an inner corner of Narrator Plantation and enter the trees to pick up the track which leads to a road. Turn right and follow the road for $^1/_2$ mile as it bends left to reach the Norsworthy Bridge car park.

POINTS OF INTEREST:

Burrator Reservoir – An attractive stretch of artificial water, built in the 1890s to supply Plymouth with drinking water. The dam is constructed of 6 ton granite blocks and holds back some one thousand million gallons of water.

Meavy – Note the ancient oak on the village green - a very photogenic spot!

Sheepstor – The church has 16th-century parts. In the churchyard is the grave of the first white Rajah of Sarawak, Sir James Brooke.

REFRESHMENTS:

The Royal Oak, Meavy.

There is sometimes an ice-cream vendor at Norsworthy.

Walk 26   KEMACOTT AND PARRACOMBE   6½m (10km)

Maps: OS Sheets Landranger 180; Outdoor Leisure 9.

A gentle walk along tracks, paths and lanes in North Devon, with distant sea views.

Start: At 685464, Martinhoe Cross, on the A39, (or at 653481, the Hunters Inn).

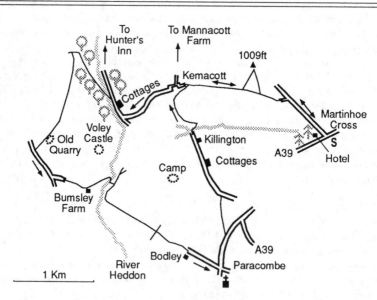

Take the lane leading north-west from Martinhoe Cross for a ¼ mile and, as it swings gently right at the edge of Martinhoe Common, bear left (westwards) along the Common's boundary, detouring if desired to the trig. point, to the right, to achieve a height of 1,000 feet (plus nine!). After a further ⅓ mile, at the hamlet and farm of **Kemacott**, keep ahead for 300 yards along the lane, following it as it turns left to reach a junction of lanes. Here turn right and, soon, right again into the wooded valley leading north to the **Hunter's Inn**. (The walk could commence at the car park just short of the inn, heading southwards to join the walk at this point.)

Just opposite some cottages on the right, leave the lane and follow a track on the left through the woods for a $^1/_3$ mile, heading northwards. On emerging from the trees, turn left and keep to the footpath as it heads south alongside several field edges for $^3/_4$ mile, passing some old quarries on the left. When a quiet lane is reached, bear left for 300 yards (the ancient camp of Voley Castle is on the high point to the left) to reach another junction. Bear left (due east) – this is the access lane to Bumsley Farm. Keep the farm to your right and, having passed it, go sharp right to ford a little brook. Now turn left, then right again, and 200 yards further on, swing left to walk along more field edges for a long $^1/_2$ mile, (south-eastwards) into the village of **Parracombe**.

Leave the village by turning left at the crossroads, with the church on your right, heading north-eastwards. Next, take the footpath veering half-left, heading due north and following the line of the old railway which used to link Barnstaple to Lynton, to reach a road. Go left, and on reaching a junction of lanes, keep half-left to pass Killington Cottages and the hamlet of Killington. When the lane goes sharply right, then left, cross the brook on the right and follow a path that bears left and then right, going around to reach Kemacott again. The route is completed by reversing the outward route back to Martinhoe Cross.

POINTS OF INTEREST:

Kemacott – From the village, a short detour of $^1/_2$ mile to the north leads to Mannacott Farm, a working farm open to the public. There are cattle, sheep etc. and a pets' corner.

Hunter's Inn – The inn is set in a thickly wooded valley with delightful short walks, including one down to the mouth of the little River Heddon.

Parracombe – Situated high on Exmoor, this village has a splendid church with fascinating interior decorations. Nearby is Holwell Castle with a motte and bailey dated to the Middle Ages.

REFRESHMENTS:

The Hunter's Inn, just off the route.
The Fox and Goose Inn, Parracombe.

Walk 27 LOWER HENDHAM AND THE AVON VALLEY 6½m (10km)

Maps: OS Sheets Landranger 202; Outdoor Leisure 20.

Through woods and fields beside the Avon, north of Kingsbridge.
Start: At 743509, the hamlet of Lower Hendham, 8m north of
Kingsbridge.

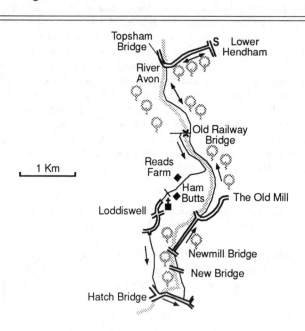

This gentle walk uses the banks of the Devon Avon, and farm tracks and field paths
near Loddiswell.

From the hamlet of Lower Hendham, take the lane westwards for ²/₃ mile
heading down the valley to the wooded banks of the Avon. As the lane swings north,
take the footpath on the left, heading southwards, with woods on the left and an **old
railway line** and the river on the right. After 1¼ miles the river swings right in a large
bend and the footpath divides: take the right fork, crossing the line and the river. Now
ignore the track heading west across the fields, taking the path heading southwards
alongside the river for a further ½ mile. The path now swings right by an ugly
corrugated iron fence, heading away from the river to follow a narrow valley and

passing to the left of Reads Farm. Ascend to Ham Butts, go over at a cross-lanes and soon take the footpath to the left, just before reaching Loddiswell church. Follow the churchyard wall, going between bungalows, and cross a road to continue along the footpath. Follow it to a road at the old school. Cross and turn right past Hillside House. Soon, bear left (Town Park) and watch out for a stile ahead as the road swings sharp right. The route beyond continues southwards across and alongside six fields (as waymarked) to a lane just short of Hatch Bridge.

Cross, turn left and after $1/4$ mile turn left by Culverwell Bridge. Now, just before Millers Path, go over a stile and walk down to the river, on the left. Follow the riverside path due north to Newmill Bridge (the second bridge). Here join the road that runs beside the river to reach the Avon Garden Centre – a short way off to the right. From the old railway station the walk now follows the disused railway, passing weirs, and going through woods and wild flowers back to the railway bridge which was crossed earlier in the walk. From here retrace your steps back to Lower Hendham.

POINTS OF INTEREST:

Old railway line – The line was victim of 'Dr Beeching's Axe' in 1963, but still has some fine items of Victorian railway architecture.

In Spring, the wild flowers on this walk are magnificent.

REFRESHMENTS:

The Loddiswell Inn, Loddiswell.
Also available at Avon Mill Garden Centre.

Walk 28　Merrivale and Great Mis Tor　6½m (10km)

Maps: OS Sheets Landranger 191; Outdoor Leisure 28.

Historic and prehistoric remains on lonely Dartmoor.

Start: At 561748, the Four Winds car park, beside the B3357 west of Princetown.

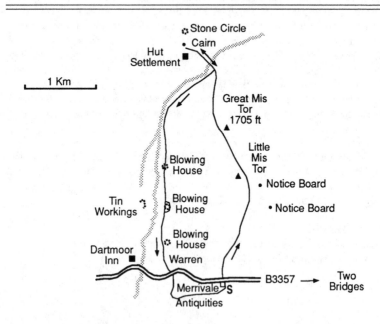

Essential requirements for this fine short walk on Dartmoor are good visibility, map and compass (plus a knowledge of how to use them) and a check on Army firing-range times (tel: 01837-52939).

From the **Car Park**, cross the B3357 and strike northwards along a clear track, passing the remnants of hut circles, to the left, and range notice boards, to the right, to reach the top of Little Miss Tor. Continue to the 1765 foot (538m) top of Great Mis Tor, some 1½ miles from the start point. The 360° panorama from the summit is a just reward for the effort of reaching it.

Now descend northwards into the valley of the River Walkham, jump/wade/ ford the stream and ascend half-left for about ¼ mile to reach a Bronze Age hut settlement, turfed but clearly visible on Langstone Moor. Retrace your steps back across the stream and head south-westwards and southwards to reach a stile into Merrivale Newtake, taking note of the medieval tin-smelting 'blowing-house' up to your left. A detour is required for a closer examination. Now follow the river southwards, passing another blowing-house and **Merrivale Warren**. Cross two streams, then climb to reach a stile on to the main road.

Cross the road into the heart of the **Merrivale Antiquities**, then head due east to return to the car park and start.

POINTS OF INTEREST:

Car Park – When the area was busy with granite quarry workings there was a school for the children of the workmen on this spot.

Merrivale Warren – Once a centre for rabbit-breeding, the grassy mounds are clear indications of where the warreners kept the rabbits before killing them for the table and coney-fur.

Merrivale Antiquities – Prehistoric stone circles, stone rows, standing stones, hut circles, cairns and a burial chamber make up this fascinating area. All the sites deserve a closer look.

REFRESHMENTS:

None on the route but *the Dartmoor Inn*, is $^3/_4$ mile west of start, and there is a good selection in Princetown.

Walk 29 MALMSMEAD AND DOONE COUNTRY 6¹/₂m (10km)

Maps: OS Sheets Landranger 180; Outdoor Leisure 9.

A walk with deep, wooded valleys, open moorland and memories of a classic tale.

Start: At 793479, the car park in Malmsmead.

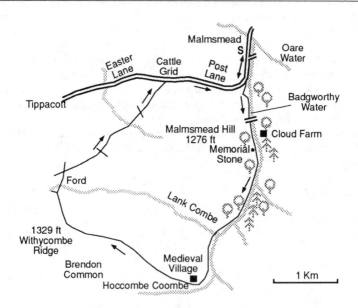

From the car park, head south along the road, passing the bridge over Badgworthy Water and keeping the stream to your left for a short ¹/₄ mile to reach a point where the road turns sharply right. Here, bear left through a gate on to a clear footpath with yellow waymarks. Follow the path for 2 miles to reach a footbridge over Lank Combe, noting, on the way, evidence of a bridge which was swept away in the great flood of 1952 which caused the disaster at nearby **Lynmouth**, and the Blackmore Memorial Stone. It is worth diverting right to explore Lank Combe - and perhaps to see a few of the very shy red deer which roam **Exmoor**. Cross the footbridge and continue southwards for another ³/₄ mile in the deep **Valley of the Doones** to reach Hoccombe Combe and its ruined medieval village, to the right.

Here, the route leaves Badgworthy Water, bearing right (westwards), following a signpost for 'Brendon Common'. Soon you bear north-westwards and uphill. The route now goes down and then up again, with Brendon Common, up to the left, to reach Lankcombe Ford where several tracks meet.

Go ahead, uphill (northwards), heading for a signpost on the skyline $^1/_4$ mile further on. Now turn right (signed for 'Malmsmead') to reach another convergence of tracks. Bear left (north-eastwards), going a little downhill for about $^1/_3$ mile to reach a ford. Maintain the north-easterly direction for a short mile to meet a lane, Post Lane, which has come from the hamlets of Tippacott and Slocombeslade, to the left. Turn right along this lane, going downhill for $^1/_2$ mile to reach the sharp turn passed on the outward leg of the walk. Now retrace the outward journey to reach the ford and bridge at Malmsmead, where refreshments are available, and the start of the walk.

POINTS OF INTEREST:

Lynmouth – A small fishing village when herring were plentiful in the Bristol Channel, Lynmouth began to attract holiday visitors in the late 1700s and, with its fine setting and the nearby coast and river valleys, became deservedly popular thereafter. In August 1952, nine inches of rain fell on Exmoor in 24 hours causing a flood in the Lyn valley which destroyed power lines, bridges, houses and caravans and drowned 31 people. Extensive precautions have since been taken to avert a repeat of such a tragedy.

Exmoor – One-third of the Exmoor National Park lies in North Devon, an area of deep valleys, high sea-cliffs, grassland and heather moors. There are red deer, wild Exmoor ponies and many relics of early man.

The Valley of the Doones – This is the setting of R D Blackmore's classic book *Lorna Doone*. It is thought that the infamous Carver Doone and his gang inhabited the now derelict village of Hoccombe Combe. The Badgworthy Water (pronounced 'Badgery') area is redolent with Doone atmosphere. The book is fiction, but based on fact and the landscape lends itself to the fine story. R D Blackmore is commemorated at the Blackmore Stone, passed on the walk.

REFRESHMENTS:

Light refreshments are available at Malmsmead, and there is a good selection of cafes, inns and restaurants in nearby Lynton and Lynmouth.

Walk 30   **NORTH TAWTON**   6¹/₂m (10km)

Maps: OS Sheets Landranger 191; Pathfinder 1294.

Easy walks along the River Taw.

Start: At 663018, The Square, North Tawton,

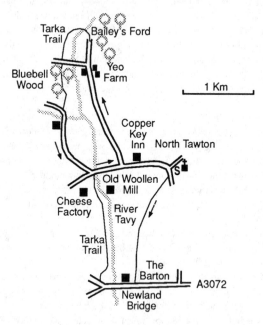

Walk southwards along the High Street, **North Tawton**, soon turning left into Barton Street. Go past the Methodist Church, to the left, the Police Station and the Memorial Park and, as the road bends right, turn right along a public footpath. Follow the path to a stile. Cross and go through fields and a gate, heading towards buildings to reach the main Crediton-Hatherleigh road (the A3072) by 'The Barton' – an old mansion. Turn right, with great care, cross the Taw and turn right again to head northwards along the river bank footpath. This path is part of the **Tarka Trail**: follow the Trail for an attractive mile of river walking to reach a road leading into North Tawton at Taw Bridge. For a shorter walk, follow the road back into the village.

The walk continues by crossing the bridge towards North Tawton but then turning left into Yeo Lane opposite Farwell House, to the right. Follow this quiet lane for a good mile, passing Yeo Farm. At a fork by a gate in the farm, take the right branch and ascend a lane. The lane becomes a track: descend it to reach the river again. Cross by Bailey's Ford (or over the original 'Bailey Bridge'?) to reach a field and go left alongside the river, heading southwards into Bluebell Wood. At the far end of the trees, go over a stile and, maintaining direction, go over a second stile. Now turn right along a short track, at the end of which turn left along a lane to Bridge Farm. Pass the farm and follow the lane for a further $1/2$ mile to reach Taw Bridge. Turn left here and follow the road to Fore Street and The Square.

POINTS OF INTEREST:

North Tawton – At the time of the Domesday recording (1086) Tawland, as it was then known, had a population of 200. St Peter's Church is mostly 15th-century though the tower dates from 200 years earlier. There was a Roman fort hereabouts and the town was an important trading centre until the beginning of the present century. Serge and other woollens were made here, there was a tannery and ginger beer was bottled.
The Tarka Trail – This long distance footpath was created for walkers to explore the countryside of North Devon as described by Henry Williamson in his famous book *Tarka the Otter*.

REFRESHMENTS:

The Copper Key, Fore Street, North Tawton. The inn was once a cock-fighting venue.

Maps: OS Sheets Landranger 192; Pathfinder 1315.

A gentle walk along riverside and across farmland. Can be muddy after rain.

Start: At 094952, the bridge over the Otter in Ottery St Mary.

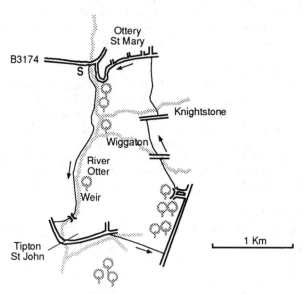

From the bridge in **Ottery St Mary**, about 9 miles north of Sidmouth, take the river bank path southwards, following the delightful Otter through meadows, sometimes muddy after recent rain, for 2 miles. Walk under an old railway bridge and turn right to join a road. Turn left and follow the road into Tipton St John. Walk through Tipton, turning left past the Golden Lion and then left again to walk eastwards out of the village. Turn right and, after a few yards, take the steps on the left, descending to a path alongside a stream, to the left. Maintain the easterly course, following a hedge to reach a stile. Cross and follow the path to a junction. Do not go right: instead, keep ahead into a farm. Ascend alongside the stream, and at the top go through a gate, to the left. Follow the bridleway beyond, going across another junction of paths and continuing to reach a lane.

Turn left, northwards, and follow the lane for a mile. Ignore a lane to the left, but turn left at the next road. Soon after, turn right down a path between houses. As this track bends left, keep right, going through a gate and across a field to a stile. Go over and follow the yellow arrow to the left, descending to some trees. Go over a stile, to the left, with a stream to the right, then another stile to reach a gate. Go through on to a road. Cross straight over and follow the path opposite. Cross a stile, to the left, and then another, heading northwards across the next field, heading for the single tree in the middle. At the tree, walk a little left and downhill to reach a road.

Turn right to the entrance to Knightstone Manor. There, turn left, passing the house and continuing northwards for almost a mile to reach the built-up area of Ottery St Mary. Turn left to reach the main road. Cross, with care, into Winter Lane, then go left into St Saviour Road and then Millcroft, going right, down the hill, to the reach main road again and the bridge.

POINTS OF INTEREST:

Ottery St Mary – This is a delightful little town of squares, lanes and streets containing 17th-century and Georgian houses. The twin-towered church is rather like a small Exeter Cathedral and is well worth a visit. If it is windy, you might hear the weathervane's cockerel whistle – two tubes in its body making it moan!

REFRESHMENTS:

The Golden Lion Inn, Tipton St John.
There is also a good selection in Ottery St Mary.

Walk 32   EAST BUDLEIGH AND OTTERTON   7m (11km)

Maps: OS Sheets Landranger 192; Pathfinder 1330.

Fairly easy coastal and footpath walk, with plenty of wild flowers and fine scenery.

Start: At 066849, East Budleigh Church.

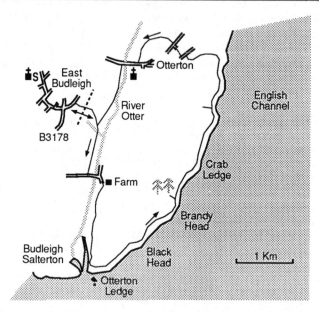

From **East Budleigh** church – the village is situated 3 miles north of Budleigh Salterton – walk south (towards Budleigh) to reach a T-junction. Turn right, and immediately left to go down to a crossroads with the B3178. Go straight over, with care, heading eastwards to where the road bends left. There, take the marked footpath on the right, soon crossing an old railway line. Follow the path as it swings around to the right to join another footpath coming in from the left. Continue southwards, now with the River Otter to your left, going through several gates as you walk for almost a mile to reach a minor road. Turn left and cross a bridge over the Otter.

On the far side of the bridge, turn right through a farm gate to reach the South Devon Coastal Path. Follow the Path southwards for $^3/_4$ mile to reach the coast itself.

Now turn left (north-north-eastwards) and follow the Coastal Path for 3 miles through splendid scenery. The Path passes Crab Ledge and Chiselbury Bay and reaches the beach at Ladram Bay. Here it is possible to bathe, purchase fresh fish and, perhaps, an ice-cream as well as to admire the red cliffs and off-shore stacks.

At Ladram Bay, turn inland along the lane to the left, but shortly take the signed footpath on the left for 'Otterton'. Follow the path for $^1/_2$ mile to join another track, going right and then left to emerge on to a lane. Go left, but after 25 yards go through the kissing gate on the right and ascend the field beyond to reach a gate. Go through and keep alongside a hedge to reach a stile. Cross and descend to a lane. Turn left and walk to a lay-by for buses, to the right. Now keep ahead, passing a cottage and then bearing left to climb to another stile. Cross into a field, then go left in the next field and over one more stile to reach a path which leads to the rear of the Kings Arms, **Otterton**.

Suitably refreshed, go right to pass or visit the mill before crossing the bridge over the Otter. Now turn left through a kissing gate and proceed southwards along the river bank for a mile.

To return to East Budleigh and the start of the walk, turn right at the path junction where on the outward journey the river bank was gained. Now retrace the outward route back to East Budleigh.

POINTS OF INTEREST:

East Budleigh – There are several cob and thatch buildings in the village, and an interesting church (be sure to see the bench ends and Walter Raleigh pew – the famous sailor was born nearby).

Otterton – This fine village has more thatched cottages, a church with blue marble columns and a roof of carved pine, and 'The Museum that Works' at Otterton Mill.

REFRESHMENTS:

The Sir Walter Raleigh Inn, East Budleigh.
The King's Arms, Otterton.

Walk 33   COTLEIGH   7m (11km)

Maps: OS Sheets Landranger 192; Pathfinder 1297.

Field paths, quiet East Devon lanes and woodland. Some steep sections and stiles.

Start: At 204022, in Cotleigh.

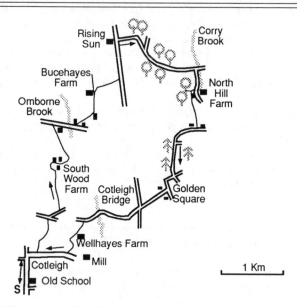

This walk offers a quiet walk in East Devon with good views into Dorset and Somerset. It begins at the old school house in Cotleigh, a scattered village about 3 miles north-east of Honiton.

Walk northwards along the lane out of the village and take the first turning right, towards Holmsleigh Green. Very soon, bear left and then immediately left through a gate into a field. Go diagonally across to reach another gate. Go through, turn right and contour around to a second field. Now head towards a single cottage (there are farm buildings off to the left).

At the cottage, which is on the Old Chard Road, turn right, but very soon fork left along a lane. Go left again at a footpath sign, into a field. Keeping a hedge to your right, walk along the edges of four fields almost as far as South Wood Farm. Turn half-left through a gate on to an access track and follow it around to the right, going between the farm and some cottages. Enter the wood ahead and turn left (north-north-westwards) to follow a path for $^1/_2$ mile. In April you will be walking through a profusion of bluebells. This path is clear at first, but does become overgrown and rough: persistence brings the determined to a lane with a house to the right and other, older houses higher up on the left. Turn right along the road, following it steeply down to cross the Umborne Brook. Now take the footpath signed diagonally left, ascending across a field. Go through a gate with yellow waymarkers and continue to Bucehayes Common, passing a house to the right.

Do not turn right along the gravel path: instead, keep left alongside a tall hedge, on your right, heading northwards for $^1/_4$ mile to reach Bucehayes Farm. Turn right along the farm access road to reach a road at Stockland Hill. Turn left and follow the road northwards for $^1/_2$ mile to reach an antique shop marked on the OS map as 'The Rising Sun'. There are no refreshments here now!

At the shop, turn right along a quiet lane, following it downhill and bearing right. Ignore another lane off to the left, going past some kennels and continue down to Corry Brook. Turn right just before the brook, following a lane for $^1/_4$ mile to reach North Hill Farm. There, turn right at a footpath sign, going up a track into woodland. Soon, bear left to walk alongside hedges, to your left, going across three fields and over two stiles and then crossing a further field to the farm buildings ahead. On emerging at a lane, turn right, ascending the lane - it becomes a track - as it bends left at the top. Ignoring other footpath signs leading right, and continue along the lane for a short $^1/_2$ mile to reach a crossroads. Turn right and ascend to Golden Square.

Keep right along the lane, still climbing, to reach the Royal Oak Cross on Stockland Hill. Go straight over and follow a lane as it descends to Cotleigh Bridge. Cross and ascend, and, soon after passing Burnside, to the right, cross into the field on the left. Go straight ahead, passing to the left of the farm buildings of Wellhayes. Follow yellow markers through two gates and then go left to reach a third. Go through and turn right along a path to reach a fourth gate. Go through and turn left along a rough path which leads to a lane where a sign shows 'The Mill' back to the left. Turn right along this quiet, sunken lane to reach the houses at Holmsleigh Green which were passed early in the walk. Turn left at the junction of lanes to return to the old school and the start.

REFRESHMENTS:
There are no opportunities to purchase refreshments en route, so take your own or drive into Honiton after completing the walk.

Maps: OS Sheets Landranger 191; Outdoor Leisure 28.
*Footpaths, moorland tracks and quiet lanes. Sometimes muddy
and boggy.*
Start: At 652727, Hexworthy, near Princeton.

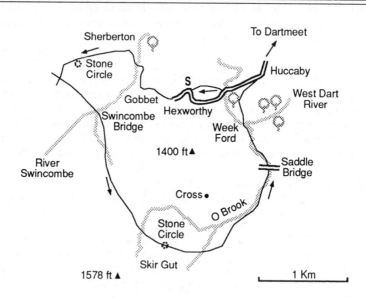

Head westward from the village of Hexworthy, going over a cattle grid towards
Sherbaton, and noting the old mines (**The Gobbet**) in the valley, below and to the
left. Soon, cross the River Swincombe and go briefly north through the farm buildings
before heading west again along the bridleway. In about ^{1}/$_4$ mile you pass the stone
circle, to the left, and then make for the enclosure corner and a signpost. Now walk
south-west for another ^{1}/$_4$ mile to reach a track junction and another signpost. Turn
left, south-east, and descend to a stile, lane and bridge at Swincombe Bridge. Cross
and head south up a gully for about a mile, bearing gently left, then cross a brook
north of Skir Gut.

Now swing more easterly, going through a small stone circle and down towards the remains of Hooten Wheals. This area is usually muddy! The pyramids are the spoil heaps of old mining activity. Press on through the boggy bits, bearing round to the left, northwards, alongside the River O. Cross the river at **Saddle Bridge,** going over the road and heading downstream to cross the West Dart via stepping stones. Now follow the waymarks to reach Huccaby Farm and a road. Turn left to reach a bridge a $^1/_4$ mile further on. Cross the bridge and immediately turn right (over a stone stile) into a field. The waymarks now clearly assist the route through a farm and through a gate. Go left along the lane to reach the Forest Inn and the starting point.

POINTS OF INTEREST:

The Gobbet – Tin has been mined in Devon and Cornwall for centuries, possibly since Phoenician, i.e. pre-Christian, times, and there is strong evidence of international trade in the metal for two thousand years. The Gobbet mine and Hooten Wheals mine are not this old but were certainly sources of industrial wealth in more recent times.

Saddle Bridge – The ruin of a power house connected with the mine workings can be seen here. The River O has the shortest place name in the country.

REFRESHMENTS:

The Forest Inn, Hexworthy.

Walk 35   STOKENHAM AND SLAPTON SANDS   7¹/₂m (12km)

Maps: OS Sheets Landranger 202; Outdoor Leisure 20.
Easy walking along paths, lanes and beach.
Start: At 807428, in Stokenham.

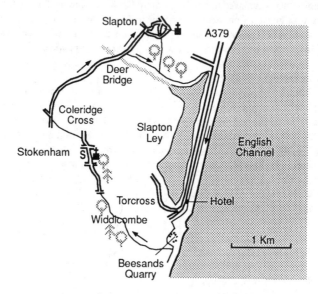

Begin between the church and the Church House Inn at Stokenham, off the A379
near Torcross: walk north and turn right just before reaching the Tradesmens' Arms
Inn. Continue uphill to Kiln Lane. Go right, and left by Kiln Cottage, and 300 yards
out of the village leave the lane along a footpath, to the left. Go across three fields,
heading north-westwards, to Coleridge Cross. There, turn right along a lane, following
it for 1¹/₄ miles, descending to Deer Bridge. About 30 yards beyond the bridge, take a
path, on the right, through the reeds (or continue up to **Slapton** village for
refreshments and then go back across the signposted fields, heading southwards – a
detour of about a mile). The reed and tree-lined path, which can be muddy after rain,
leads, after ³/₄ mile, to a junction. Here the route continues into the Nature Reserve, to
the right, going partly along board-walks, skirting Slapton Ley and crossing Slapton
Bridge to reach the A379 and, beyond (cross with care) the beach at **Slapton Sands**.

Now either follow the footpath which runs south alongside the Ley, or walk along the shingle beach for $1\frac{1}{2}$ miles to reach the hamlet of **Torcross** where refreshments may well be necessary before attempting the steep steps beyond the Torcross Hotel. After the steps, follow the winding path up above Beesands Quarry, before descending steeply seawards. Now look for, and take, the signed footpath heading westwards to 'Widdicombe'. Follow the path over stiles and into woodland. Pass two cottages to reach the junction of three tracks. Keep right and after a further 80 yards you will reach a signed footpath to 'Widewell'. Do not take this: instead, after a further 12 yards, go through a kissing gate into a field. Cross this to reach a lane, going ahead to descend this for $\frac{1}{2}$ mile to reach its junction with main A379. Cross with care: the Church House Inn at Stokenham and the start are ahead.

POINTS OF INTEREST:
Slapton – The village was one of very many in the area evacuated during the 1939-45 war to provide a training area for troops preparing for the Normandy Invasion. The nearby Ley is the largest freshwater area in Devon – a migratory stop-over where many water birds may be seen.
Slapton Sands – A memorial and a tank recovered from the sea reminds visitors of the sad event when 749 US troops died during D-Day rehearsals in 1944.
Torcross – This tiny village has a new seawall following recent violent storms. Torcross is an attractive fishing and holiday village.

REFRESHMENTS:
The Church House Inn, Stokenham.
The Tradesmens' Arms, Stokenham.
The Tower Inn, Slapton.
Start Bay Inn, Torcross – where the speciality is fish and chips!

Walk 36   OTTERY ST MARY AND EAST HILL   7¹/₂m (12km)
Maps: OS Sheets Landranger 192; Pathfinder 1315.
Riverbank, farmland and wooded ridge - fairly easy, but may be muddy.
Start: At 095955, the Land of Canaan car park, Ottery St Mary.

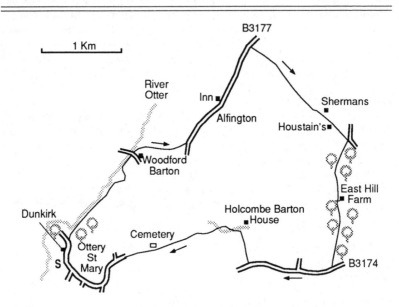

From the quaintly-named car park in **Ottery St Mary**, turn left (northwards) away from the town, following the road which passes Dunkirk Cottages. When the road turns left to cross the river, walk straight ahead on a path through a copse. Maintain direction (northerly), later heading north-eastwards, with the delightful River Otter never far off to the left. The footpath is fairly well marked, with yellow arrows or blobs of paint, sometimes up 10-15 feet above the water meadow level, sometimes on the water's edge. Birds and butterflies abound, and occasionally trout leap from the river. After about a mile the bridge by Woodford Barton farm comes into view: go through a gate on to a road and turn right for a few yards. Now turn left, cross the road and go directly ahead, passing to the left of farm buildings. Follow the clear track as it swings around to the right, continuing for about ¹/₂ mile to reach the busy B3177.

Turn left, facing oncoming traffic and walking with care, to follow the road into the village of Alfington, with its welcoming inn. Continue along the B3177 for a further $1/3$ mile and, shortly after passing Bowhay, to the right, take a signed footpath, also on the right. Aim for a metal gate to the left of the small hilltop ahead. Go through and follow the track beyond for almost 2 miles, heading south-eastwards and passing close to Sherman's Farm, to the left, and Houstain's restored thatch, to the right. The track becomes stony and ascends steeply towards the woods ahead. At the top turn right – do not go through the gate into the field on the right, nor go ahead along the metalled road – to walk southwards for about $1^1/2$ miles, passing close to East Hill Farm.

On reaching a road (the B3174 at Chineway Hill) turn right, with care, and descend steeply towards Ottery St Mary. About $3/4$ mile from the top, turn right along a signed bridlepath, on the right, following it for $1/3$ mile to reach Holcombe Barton House. Just short of the house, turn left, following yellow waymarkers to cross a little stream twice. Now descend through fields towards the church ahead. The path becomes a gravel track, then a lane as it passes by the cemetery and ultimately reaches Ottery. When the B3177 is reached, turn left, descending all the while, into the town. The car park can now be found around to the right.

POINTS OF INTEREST:

Ottery St Mary – Samuel Taylor Coleridge, the poet was born here in 1772, the son of the vicar of St Mary's Church. The village was burnt down almost totally in 1866 following a very hot summer, the disaster even being reported in London! Lace and serge were produced here. It was highly-prized in Europe, much being exported.

REFRESHMENTS:

The Alfington Inn, Alfington.
There are numerous possibilities in Ottery St Mary.

Walks 37 & 38   BIGBURY AND ERME MOUTH   8m (13km)
or $11^{1}/_{2}$m (18km)

Maps: OS Sheets Landranger 202; Pathfinder 1362.
One – or rather two – of the great walks of South Devon.
Start: At 652443, Bigbury-on-Sea.

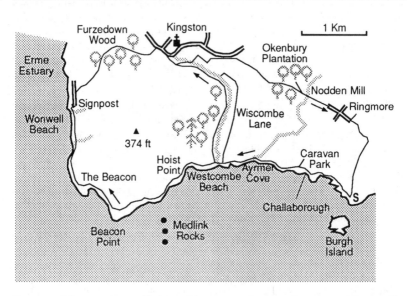

Because of the many steep climbs and descents on the coastal sections of these walks they should only be attempted by the fit and determined. The rewards are fantastic – superb scenery and fine walking inland.

From **Bigbury-on-Sea**, walk westwards along a section of the South Devon Coastal Path, passing the large caravan sites at Challaborough and the beach at Ayrmer Cove, where it is tempting to cool off with a paddle. Go over a footbridge, climb and then go down to Westcombe Beach.

The short walk turns right here, heading inland either with the stream on the right, or following the Wiscombe Lane track, with the stream to the left. Go up the steep valley, passing several long lakes, for almost 2 miles to reach a lane in the village of Kingstone, with its fine church and welcoming inn, the Dolphin. Here, the longer walk is rejoined.

The long walk continues along the Coastal Path, passing Hoist Point, Gutterslide Beach and The Beacon before opening out to Erme Mouth and descending to Wonwell Beach. Keep to the River Erme's bank, then go over a stream and down steps to join a tarmac road. Soon, turn right, ascending and obeying the signpost for 'Kingston'. Go through Furzedown Wood, bearing left at a waymarker to leave the woodland. Go over a stile and, keeping a hedge to the right, go for a second stile – the heading is a little north of east. Maintain direction across fields (there are some waymarkers) and over stiles to reach a road. Turn right to Kingston, the Dolphin Inn and the shorter walk.

To continue, do not go downhill along the road (eastwards): instead, take the little lane southwards. This quickly peters out as it approaches a stream and the top lake: after the houses on the right cease, look out for a footpath crossing the stream, heading south-eastwards, then uphill to reach a field-corner. Go up the left-hand edge of the next field, right at the next corner, then left and right again, following the field-edges, with the buildings of Okenbury below and off to the right. Cross the lane leading right, into Okenbury, following the sign for Ringmore which leads you to the right of a concrete building. The direction is southwards now: go through a plantation, over a stream near Nodden Mill and follow yellow waymarkers, going over stiles and then through a kissing gate to reach the village of Ringmore. Just past the church, go right and at once left, signposted Challaborough. Go past the Post Office, still heading south-eastwards, and descend steeply beside fields. Cross a minor road and the field beyond, then go along the right edges of two further fields. Now cross a fourth field to reach a junction of paths. Turn right and walk down into Bigbury to regain the start.

POINTS OF INTEREST:
Bigbury-on-Sea – This little seaside resort has a tidal causeway to Burgh Island. Did Agatha Christie have this in mind when she wrote *Ten Little Niggers*?

REFRESHMENTS:
The Dolphin Inn, Kingston.
The Journey's End, Ringmore.
The Pilchard Inn, on the island, Bigbury.

Walk 39   ARLINGTON AND BRATTON FLEMING   8m (13km)

Maps: OS Sheets Landranger 180; Pathfinder 1234.
A quiet inland walk in North Devon.
Start: At 613407, the village church, Arlington.

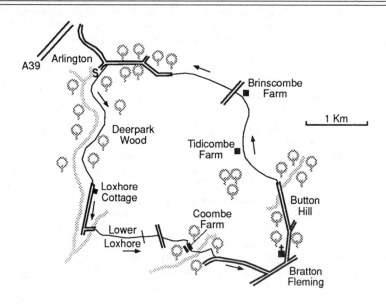

Begin the walk from the front of the church at **Arlington**, off A39 south of Combe Martin. Go through the wooden gate into the National Trust Estate. Just inside, turn right, but soon go left through The Wildness and past the lily pond. Descend and follow the signed path for 'Smallacombe Bridge'. Go over a bridge and then left through the valley. Go over Tucker's Bridge, then through Deerpark, heading southwards, with the stream, to Loxhore Cottage. Maintain direction, going through iron gates to reach a road. Go ahead for about 250 yards, then go left along a bridleway, following it uphill to reach a lane. Turn right turn into **Lower Loxhore**.

At the chapel, turn left, ascend and then go right along a bridleway. This descends, goes straight over a crossing track and continues to reach a lane. Go right, but almost at once take the left fork at a junction, following a bridlepath to Coombe Farm. The path turns right, goes through the farm buildings and then through a little wood, heading downhill alongside a stream. Cross the stream and go steeply up to reach a road. Turn left into **Bratton Fleming**.

Walk past St Peter's Church (northwards) and take the left fork (Button Hill). Descend to cross the old railway line and, by keeping left, the stream at Button Bridge. On the far side, take the keep right track, going along the valley and then climbing up to Tidicombe Farm. Keep just to the right of the farm buildings, following helpful yellow waymarkers across fields to Brinscombe Farm. Here, bear left along the access drive to reach a lane at the highest point in the walk (797 feet – 243m). Now take the bridleway immediately opposite, heading downhill to woodland and continuing due west to reach a minor road. Follow this past an old school to reach a junction. Keep left, then go left again to return to the church.

POINTS OF INTEREST:

Arlington – Arlington Court is now a National Trust property, open to the public. It boasts a splendid Regency Saloon, fine silken boudoirs, mahogany furniture, a William Blake watercolour and a collection of 19th-century carriages as well as many other treasures. In the village's 15th-century church is a monument to the last private owner of the Court, designed by John Piper.

Loxhore – This is a very scattered village, the map shows Lower Loxhore, Loxhore Cott and Loxhore Town. Today it houses commuters to Barnstaple in modern houses and bungalows, a sharp contrast to the 16th-century cottages.

Bratton Fleming – This large village has an old, restored church with a set of old bell clappers. Between Loxhore and the village is the almost hidden ruin of Castle Roborough.

REFRESHMENTS:
The White Hart, Bratton Fleming.
There is a Tea Rooms in Arlington.

Walk 40   HARTLAND POINT   8m (13km)

Maps: OS Sheets Landranger 190; Pathfinder 1253.

One of the great North Devon coast walks, with demandingly steep sections and quiet inland paths.

Start: At 235274, Hartland Point car park.

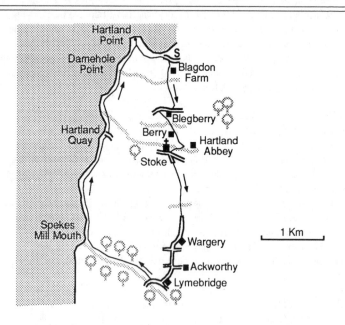

From the car park at **Hartland Point** walk south along the lane leading to Blagdon Farm. Go through the farm buildings and keep south along a bridleway, heading downhill at first, then going over a stream and climbing up between the typical earth covered walls to reach a lane. Turn right to reach Blegberry and turn left there, heading south again to reach Berry, another farm. The farm lane now heads south-east, descending to cross the Abbey River. Hartland Abbey is a short detour to the left, here.

The walk continues uphill to reach the hamlet of **Stoke**. Keep heading southwards, passing the church, to the right, and going along the lane opposite for a long mile to reach a crossing of lanes just past Wargery. Keep ahead to reach the next crossing, at Lymebridge. Turn right. Now, as the track ends at two gates, keep left, following a signpost for 'Speke's Mill Mouth'. Go over a stile, and, heading westward towards the coast, pass Speke's Mill Cottage and continue along the deep and scenic little valley to the sea. The river plunges 70 feet to the beach here, making it an excellent place to pause, take photographs and even cool off warm feet or bathe before tackling the cliff climbs and descents.

To continue, turn right and go steeply up the Coastal Path, enjoying the fine scenery – Lundy Island is 11 miles northwards – and the birds. Continue along the Coastal Path, going up and down for another long mile to reach the hotel at **Hartland Quay**. From the hotel, continue northwards along the Coastal Path, which still offers very strenuous walking with the compensation of spectacular formations of cliffs, rocks, stream-mouths and shelving beaches. Eventually the Path swings right on to a road. A short detour left here will take you to Hartland Point and its lighthouse, while the road, heading eastwards, brings the walk back to the start.

POINTS OF INTEREST:
The dramatic coast scenery predominates on this splendid walk through North Devon, though the footpaths, usually bordered by wild flowers and embellished with bird-song, have their own charm too.

Hartland Point – The Point, with its savage rocky shoreline, is Devon's Land's End. Lundy and the coast of South Wales far off to the north dominate the far view from the lighthouse perched on top of the 325 foot cliff.
Stoke – The village church has a fine tower, 15th-century rood screen and a wagon roof. The nearby ruined abbey is open to the public to view furniture and porcelain.
Hartland Quay – Once an important harbour, but now just a grand viewpoint and a welcome break with its interesting museum, worth visiting for 'local colour'.

REFRESHMENTS:
Hartland Point and Hartland Quay both cater for thirsty walkers with hotels and cafés serving cream teas etc.

Walk 41   **BELLEVER AND POSTBRIDGE**   8m (13km)

Maps: OS Sheets Landranger 191; Outdoor Leisure 28.

A forest and open moorland walk – easy, but take care if misty.

Start: At 656773, the car park in Bellever Forest.

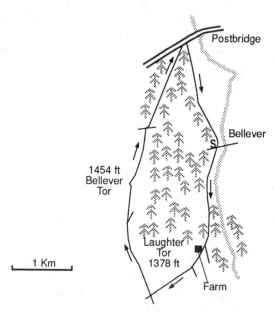

From the Forestry Commission's **Bellever Forest** car park, just south of the Bellever Youth Hostel, walk south along the signposted forest walk. Maintain this southerly course uphill along a bridleway (not along the right fork) to reach a gate. Beyond the gate, the path continues uphill, with the East Dart River down to the left, for a mile, as the forest opens into fields. Continue southwards back into the forest again, forking right to reach Laughter Hole Farm. Continue through the pine forest, going uphill to reach the signpost 'B3357' at Huccaby Cottage. Now keep straight on, going through gates and following the next sign 'to Dunnsbridge Pound'. The path contours Laughter Tor (the highest point, 1378 feet – 420m – is off to the right), swinging south-westwards and passing an ancient stone row, to the right. At a clear crossing of footpaths, turn right and follow the signed track for Bellever Tor.

The track is not clear at first, so aim directly for the Tor, north-westwards, and after about $^3/_4$ mile you will reach a gate where three walls meet at the edge of the forest. Follow the signed path to the Tor again, heading due north now, with a wall to the right. A very short detour off to the left reaches the Tor's summit at 1454 feet (443m), from where the views are splendid. Continue by heading due north, following the red-banded posts for $^3/_4$ mile to where a bridlepath crosses the oath. Turn right and very soon left to return to the forest again. The Forestry Commission's track runs clearly now, taking you due north and downhill for $1^1/_2$ miles (ignore all crossing tracks) to reach the B3212. Turn right, with care, towards **Postbridge** and its clapper bridge.

A few yards west of the bridge and inn at Postbridge, turn right along a bridleway signed to Bellever. Continue with the river down to your left, going through a gate and ascending alongside a wall, to the left. When the bridleway joins a forestry road, follow the road south-eastwards to the hamlet of Bellever. Cross straight over the road (another clapper bridge is just off to the left) to enter the forest once more, soon arriving back at the start.

POINTS OF INTEREST:

Bellever Forest – There are many alternative routes through this forest which was planted with conifers in the 1920s to produce quick growing timber. Leaflets on the possibilities are available at the car park.

Postbridge – The famous clapper bridge – huge slabs of granite sitting on buttresses of more granite – was erected to enable pack-horses to cross the Dart in medieval times. The Dartmoor National Park has an information centre in the hamlet.

REFRESHMENTS:

Postbridge has an inn, shops and, often, an ice-cream van in the summer.

Walk 42 DITTISHAM 8½m (14km)

Maps: OS Sheets, Landranger 202; Outdoor Leisure 20.
Tidal creeks, field paths, tracks and quiet lanes, with fine views.
Start: At 862519, Old Mill Bridge, north-west of Dartmouth.

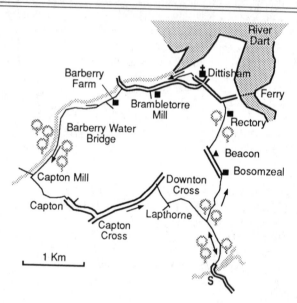

Begin by taking the track (often muddy) from the lime kiln above the boatyards, heading eastwards, then ascending northwards towards Lapthorne Farm. After ½ mile, go through a metal gate to the right, and cross a little bridge. Follow the signposted bridleway through a little wood, then go through another gate into fields. On reaching a road, turn left and pass Bosomzeal and **Fire Beacon Hill** (514 metres). After passing the summit, cross a stile in the hedge on the right into a field, and continue downhill (north-eastwards), making for the trees and buildings of Lower Dittisham. On reaching the track by the Rectory, bear left and follow it around to a junction (Manor Road). Turn right here for a short detour to where refreshments can be found by the ferry.

The walk continues uphill to reach **Dittisham** and the Red Lion Inn. Cross Riverside Road, descend the steps on the right, and follow the path, to the left, around the creek. (If the tide is high the upper road will have to be used instead.) The path and road meet up near Brambletorre Mill, from where the walk continues to Coombe Farm Studios. Turn left here, passing Barberry Farm. Now, when the lane turns sharp left, go straight on for about 50 yards to reach the next junction. Again keep straight on, going above the little stream to curve round for a short $^1/_2$ mile walk to Barberry Water Bridge. Just before the bridge, go through the gate on the left, and follow the signed path up into the woods and on to Capton Mill. Turn left past the mill and ascend to the Village of **Capton**.

Continue south-eastwards for another $^1/_2$ mile to reach Capton Cross. Turn left along the lane towards Dittisham, and after a further $^1/_2$ mile, at Downton Cross, turn right through the farm and, just before a right-hand bend in the track, turn left along the left edge of a signed field. Now go left and right, through trees and the buildings of Lapthorne, then continue south-eastwards for a long $^1/_4$ mile, dropping down to meet the outward route. Now reverse the outward route back to the start.

POINTS OF INTEREST:
Fire Beacon Hill – The name derives from the great bonfire lit to warn of the approach of the Spanish Armada in 1588.
Dittisham – The name is pronounced Ditsum. This fine village of stone and thatch has an excellent old church boasting a Norman font and 15th-century carved pulpit.
Capton – A Prehistoric Settlement Museum here is open daily during summer months.

REFRESHMENTS:
The Red Lion Inn, Dittisham.
The Ferryboat Inn, Dittisham.
There is also a café in Dittisham.

Walk 43 DARTMOUTH CASTLE AND STOKE FLEMING $8\frac{1}{2}$m (14km)

Maps: OS Sheets Landranger 202, Outdoor Leisure 20.

Channel views, tracks and lanes, and 'Strawberry Valley'. Can be muddy.

Start: At 886503, Dartmouth Castle, south of Dartmouth and Warfleet.

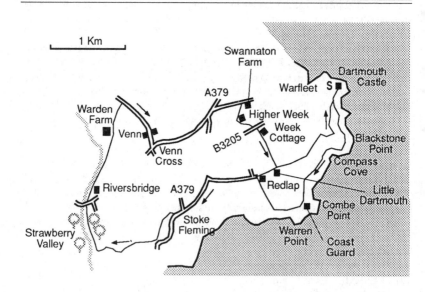

From the road above **Dartmouth Castle**, walk southwards towards the cottages above Compass Cove following the sign directing you left to Blackstone Point. Keep to the South Devon Coastal Path above the wave-cut platform and Compass Cove (where swimming is possible!) and go over a stile into a shallow valley. Now climb to a waymarker and go left. Stay up on the cliff path, keeping inland at the coastguard lookout, and after a short $\frac{1}{4}$ mile, above Warren Point, turn right through a kissing gate, leaving the coast and continuing to Redlap. On reaching a lane, turn left and stay on it for $\frac{3}{4}$ mile to reach the A379 on the outskirts of **Stoke Fleming**.

Turn left, with care, but soon go right into Ravensbourne Lane. Now go right again into Ven Lane, then left through white gates and swing left between wire fences. The path leads to the village inn: turn right, cross the car park and then go left on to a bridleway which descends to reach a lane. Turn right and walk northwards, passing Blackpool Farm and Embridge Mills. Turn right at Embridge Cross and soon, at Riversbridge Farm, follow a sign, left, to the bottom of the wood ahead. Now, keeping the stream on your left and a wood on your right, ascend towards Worden Farm. On reaching a gate leading into a sunken lane follow it, ascending beyond the farm to reach a T-junction.

Turn right, following the lane past Venn to reach Venn Cross. Here the walk continues left for $\frac{1}{2}$ mile to reach the main road again. Cross left, with great care, and immediately go right (eastwards) along a lane going back to Warfleet. Descend for a short $\frac{1}{4}$ mile, then turn right, just before Swannaton Farm, to go through Higher Week. After a further 400 yards, turn left (along the B3205) and then very soon right (with Week Cottage on the left). Walk alongside three field edges to the reach the buildings of Little Dartmouth. Here, swing left (eastwards), along a bridleway which will take you back to the castle and the start.

POINTS OF INTEREST:

Dartmouth Castle – Building was begun here in 1481 to assist in the defence of the harbour entrance against possible attacks from the French. Additionally, a chain was stretched across to Gommerock Castle on the eastern side – at a cost of £30! The church next to the castle, dedicated to St Petrox, has fine 17th-century brasses.

Stoke Fleming – The church has some very old brass and a fine memorial to John Corp dated 1350.

REFRESHMENTS:

The Green Dragon, Stoke Fleming.
There is a café at Dartmouth Castle and a wide choice of refreshments in Dartmouth.

Walk 44   **YARCOMBE AND STOCKLAND**   8$\frac{1}{2}$m (14km)

Maps: OS Sheets Landranger 192; Pathfinder 1297.

Fine East Devon farmland walking: gentle hills and quiet lanes,
but many gates and stiles.

Start: At 246082, Yarcombe, on the A30 north east of Honiton.

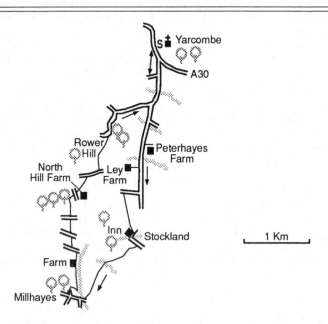

From the church, dedicated to St John, in **Yarcombe**, walk south, with great care,
towards Chard. After a short $\frac{1}{4}$ mile, keep right at a fork, then go left at a junction,
walking southwards. Ignore further junctions, both right and left, but after about
1$\frac{1}{4}$ miles, having passed the access tracks to the farms of Peterhayes and Ley, turn
right and head downhill, westward, for a further $\frac{1}{4}$ mile. Now take a footpath on the
right to head southwards again, crossing fields to arrive in the hamlet of **Stockland** and
its welcome inn, the King's Arms.

Continue down to the church, turning left, then right and, as the lane divides,
keep left, by the farm (often muddy!). The direction is now due west: go
uphill at first, crossing over a little brook, then head downhill (south-westwards)

towards the buildings at Millhayes. On reaching a lane, turn right, but almost at once go left through buildings and cross a stream. At the fork, keep hard right, then, very soon, go right again. Turn left, with the stream now on the right. Walk northwards, going between the next farm's buildings and the stream. On emerging at a lane, keep straight on, <u>not</u> left. The north-westwards direction is maintained, following footpaths across fields towards a wooded area just to the left of North Hill Farm. Bear right along the farm track, but very soon take the signed path to the left, following the waymarks to reach another lane.

Turn right for about 50 yards, then, as the lane bends right, take the access path on the left, going between buildings and so across the rise and fall of Rower Hill, heading northwards for a short mile. Now pass to the left of a wooded area, cross a little stream and emerge on to a lane at a bend. Keep walking northwards along the lane, following it around right and left bends. At a junction, keep right, then turn left at the next junction and retrace the first $^1/_4$ mile of the outward journey.

POINTS OF INTEREST:

Yarcombe – The church has some fine carving, bench ends depicting praying (thinking?) monks, animals and some angels in Elizabethan costume. There is a 'breeches' bible (see Gen. III.7) and a 14th-century glass window high in the north window picturing a pedlar with his rucsac of goodies.

Sir Francis Drake was a landowner in the Yarcombe area.

Stockland – The area has been settled since Stone Age Man, evident from the many axes and other tools he left hereabouts. More recently there have been Iron Age camps. The church – which seems very large for such a small village – is much newer, but has pre-14th-century foundations. Smugglers once used the village as a store for their contraband, even though the sea is twelve miles away!

REFRESHMENTS:
The King's Arms, Stockland.
The Village Inn, Yarcombe.

Walk 45 BUCKFASTLEIGH MOOR AND RYDER'S HILL $8^1/_2$m (14km)
Maps: OS Sheets Landranger 202; Outdoor Leisure 28.
An easy moorland walk requiring compass and clear weather.
Start: At 705695, Holne Church.

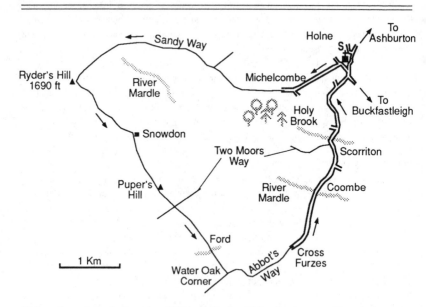

Although a relatively 'easy' walk this walk should not be attempted in mist.

Holne lies 4 miles north-west of Buckfastleigh: starting from the church, walk south for a short $^1/_4$ mile, turning right at the first junction of lanes. Now go left along Michelcombe Lane, following it for almost a mile to reach the hamlet itself. Keep straight on, westwards, along the bridleway at the western end of the hamlet. Go through a gate and out on to the gorse and bracken covered moor. Continue uphill, the track – known locally as Sandy Way – soon becoming clearer. Go past bushes and cairns as you follow the track for at least $1^1/_2$ miles, heading in a generally westerly direction before bearing left. Do not drop down to the often boggy land near the River Mardle. Now aim for the top of Ryder's Hill with its cairn (at 1690 foot – 515m) and stone pillar (Petre's Bound Stone).

Now swing left, south-eastwards, along a wider track, going gently down and then up a little to reach Snowdon a further mile on. Continue to a second rise (Puper's Hill) about $^3/_4$ mile further along the same south-easterly course. Maintain direction, going gently downhill. Soon, the Two Moors Way crosses the path: keep ahead, circumventing some boggy bits and fording a brook. Continue in the same direction to reach a group of pine trees at Water Oak Corner. Here the Abbot's Way crosses the route. Bear left with it, going through a gate and crossing waymarked fields. Go over a stream and continue to reach a lane at Cross Furzes. Turn left along the lane, following it northwards for 2 miles through the villages of Combe and Scorriton. The lanes are usually quiet and traffic-free but care is required. Beyond Scorriton the lane continues to Holne, where this gentle and rewarding walk concludes.

POINTS OF INTEREST:

Holne – Charles Kingsley was born and baptised here: his father was curate in charge at the village church of St Mary the Virgin. Tin and copper were once mined locally and the village probably served as a resting place for pack-horse trade across the moor, the pack-horses following what is now called Abbots Way.

Though not on the walk, Buckfastleigh Abbey is close to Holne and is a 'must' for the visitor.

REFRESHMENTS:

The Church House Inn, Holne.
The Tradesman's Arms, Scorriton.
There is also a café and a store in Holne.

Walk 46   **SIDBURY**   9m (14$\frac{1}{2}$km)

Maps: OS Sheets Landranger 192; Pathfinder 1315.

Wooded paths, fields and quiet lanes north of Sidmouth. Some steep sections.

Start: At 139917, the car park in the village of Sidbury.

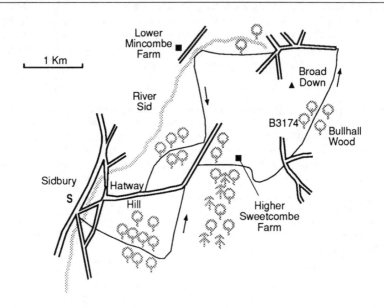

Leaving the car park in the village of **Sidbury**, 5 miles north of Sidmouth, turn right, with care, along the main road, passing the church of St Giles and St Peter and then turning left into Bridge Street. Go over the bridge and continue to a junction. Take the footpath opposite, going over a stile and across a field to reach a gate in the top left corner. Go through and walk alongside the hedge to reach another stile. Cross this and the next field to reach woodland.

     Go ahead (eastwards), steeply ascending to emerge on to open moorland and then veer left (north-eastwards) along the contour to reach a road. Turn right, then follow the sign, to the right, at Higher Sweetcombe, for 'Blackberry Castle'. Follow the drive to the third gate, then descend, with trees to the right, to reach a stile into a

92

wood of conifers and deciduous trees. Go through this mixed woodland, crossing two streams and, often, boggy ground. On reaching some old tumbledown buildings, turn right up to a broad clear track, and follow this as it turns left to a road (the B3174). With care, go straight over (not left or right!) to reach a gap in the hedge. Go through and walk north-eastwards along the field edge to reach more woodland. The path just inside the woodland leads to Little Wiscombe, with the summit of Broad Down to the left. Go through two gates to finally emerge on to a lane.

Turn left along the lane for about $1/_4$ mile to reach a junction. Go left and walk to the main road (B3174). Cross, with care, and follow the lane opposite. Soon, turn right along a footpath which leads half-left across a field, then descends, westwards, across more fields to reach Lower Mincombe Farm.

However, before reaching the lane at the farm, take the stony path which goes steeply up (south-south-eastwards), waymarked clearly to another road. Again just short of the road, turn right and continue for a $1/_4$ mile to reach a stile into woodland. On emerging, maintain the south-south-westward direction, going over a stile and through several gates to reach a road. Turn right down Hatway Hill to return to the village.

POINTS OF INTEREST:

Sidbury – This fine village rewards an easy stroll around. The church has some Saxon parts and additions of Norman and other styles – see the description at the rear of the south aisle.

REFRESHMENTS:

The Sidbury Arms, Sidbury.

Walk 47   BRAUNTON AND HALSINGER   9m (14¹/₂km)

Maps: OS Sheets Landranger 180; Pathfinder 1213.

A big field, an estuary, green lanes and fine views. There is also a 500 foot climb.

Start: At 487365, in Braunton.

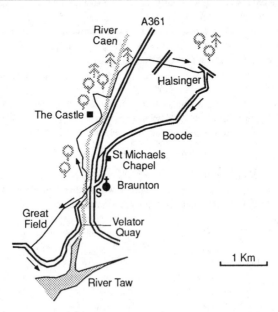

From the car park in the centre of **Braunton**, turn left, southwards, then turn left into Field Lane. Go right just past the Sea Scouts headquarters, following a track across the **Great Field** for almost a mile. The walk continues by turning left along a lane and then soon goes left again along the River Caen. Having gone past the now almost deserted Velator Quay, cross a bridge and disused railway line and walk into the built-up part of the town, returning to the car park.

This time, go ahead to the traffic lights. Turn left and, about 120 yards further on, go left through the library car park. At the end, go left to cross the river and the old railway track once again. (Keep a look out for the one-time signal box, now a greenhouse). Continue to reach the main road with a church hall opposite. Go left for

94

200 yards, then left again along a footpath. Cross a stile and walk diagonally right, descending to the right corner of the field beyond. On reaching the main A361, cross, with great care, and go left. Soon, take the track heading eastwards (opposite a house with a tall pole in the garden), following it for about $1^1/_4$ miles to reach a junction of lanes. Turn right, southwards, admiring the views of Dartmoor ahead, Exmoor to the left, and, if the weather is kind, Lundy Island 20 miles away to the right. Follow the lane, maintaining the south-westward direction, through the hamlets of Halsinger and Boode, continuing to pass to the right of St Michael's Chapel.

When Braunton is reached, continue to the end of Silver Street and past the New Inn to go into the churchyard. Turn left into the town centre and go right at the traffic lights to find the car park at the walk's end.

POINTS OF INTEREST:

Braunton – The town has a little museum reflecting the local farming and seafaring history. St Brannock's Church, largely 13th-century, has a Norman tower, interesting and amusing bosses on the wagon roof, carved bench ends and other unusual features. Visitors should discover why one boss has a sow plus her piglets carved thereon – clue: St Brannoc's dream.

The north-eastern part of the town contains old, balconied and thatched houses and, at Velator, signs of a once-thriving port where cider, apples and potatoes were sent out while coal, grain, fertiliser and limestone came in.

Great Field – In Saxon times the land here was cleared and cultivated. The area was divided into three fields and each year one was left fallow, for grazing and manuring, while the other two grew crops. Every landowner had several strips scattered about the fields so no-one had an unfair share of the best, most fertile land, but all had their due allocation. There are some 140 strips at Braunton now, but originally there were more than 650 separated by drainage ditches. The Strip System lasted many hundred years – a true co-operative!

REFRESHMENTS:

The New Inn, Braunton.

There are many other possibilities in Braunton, including Quires famous fish and chips.

Walk 48　UMBERLEIGH AND CHITTLEHAMPTON　9m (14$\frac{1}{2}$km)

Maps: OS Sheets Landranger 180; Pathfinder 1255.

A longish walk along North Devon lanes to visit three lovely villages.

Start: At 606237, the Rising Sun Inn, Umberleigh.

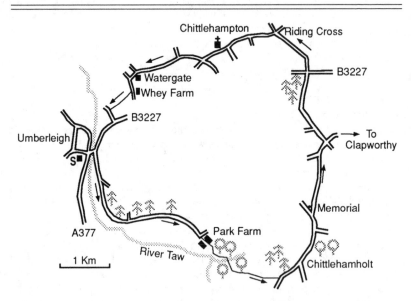

From the Rising Sun Inn, in the village of **Umberleigh**, which lies on the A377 about 6 miles south of Barnstaple, head towards the railway station and the River Taw, to reach a T-junction. Turn right and walk southwards, over a level-crossing. Continue for a further $\frac{1}{4}$ mile to reach a junction. Keep right along the road as it follows the river, swinging eastwards through woods for almost 2 miles to reach a sharp left turn. Here, go forward along the access lane to Park Farm. Go through the farm and continue for another mile along a clear track to reach its junction with a lane. Turn left and follow the lane into Chittlehamholt. In the hamlet, turn left (northwards) at the crossroads and follow a lane for a mile to reach a fork at a memorial.

Take the right branch, following the lane for $^3/_4$ mile to reach a junction. Turn right here, then left at the next junction. Keep right at the next junction and follow the lane to its junction with the B3227. Cross, with great care, and follow the lane opposite to Riding Cross. Here turn left (westwards) to reach the village of **Chittlehampton** and its welcoming inn. Maintain the westerly course through the village, passing the church, to the right, to reach a lane fork. Take the right branch, out of the village, but then turn left, downhill, passing Watergate, to the left. Keep left at two more lane junctions to reach Whey Farm, also to the left.

Take the footpath opposite, going across fields, downhill, to reach a lane. Turn left and follow the lane to its junction with the B3227. Turn right, with great care, and follow the road to reach the railway station. Turn right, then right again to return to the start.

POINTS OF INTEREST:

Chittlehampton – St Urith gives her name to the church in this fine village. On the 8th July each year a procession marks her martyrdom (she was cut to pieces with scythes) going from the lych-gate to the well where she is supposed to have fallen. A blessing, hymns and flowers complete the ceremony, which has been celebrated since the 8th century. The village has many fine porched and thatched cottages to admire and a good inn.

Umberleigh – The village is at the centre of farmland, now livestock and arable, once famous for cherry orchards. The nearby River Taw has trout and salmon to entice the angler, and was the setting for *Salar the Salmon*, Henry Williamson's 'other' masterpiece. The whole valley hereabouts is a delight to the walker, photographer, cyclist and naturalist.

REFRESHMENTS:

The Rising Sun Inn, Umberleigh.
The Bell Inn, Chittlehampton.
There are numerous possibilities in Barnstaple, to the north, and South Molton, to the east, as well as a tea shop in Umberleigh and another inn in Chittlehamholt.

Walk 49   STEPS BRIDGE TO MARDON DOWN   9m (14½km)

Maps: OS Sheets Landranger 191, Outdoor Leisure 28.

A justifiably popular walk through wonderful woodland on the edge of Dartmoor.

Start: At 803884, Steps Bridge Youth Hostel.

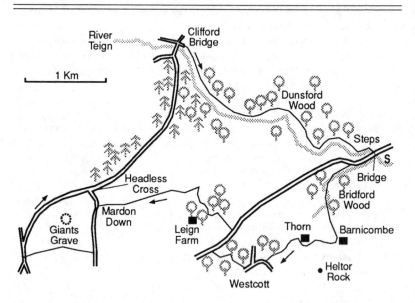

Breezy open moorland, deciduous and pine forests, and wild flowers all combine to make this walk a 'special'. Go mid-week if possible.

   Begin at the Youth Hostel near Dunsford, a few miles north-east of Moretonhampstead, where there is a Park Centre car park. Cross the road and take the path for Burnicombe (waymarked by blue dots) and ascend through Bridford Wood, crossing a little bridge and walking alongside the stream before crossing again, this time by stepping-stones. Beyond the river, the way is south-west at first, but then turns more southerly to emerge from the forest. Cross the stream once again and follow waymarkers through fields for a further ¼ mile to reach the farmyard at Burnicombe. Here, turn right with a hedge (on your right) and walk alongside a field to reach a gate. Now with the hedge on your left walk along the next field edge to reach a stile on the left. Cross this on to a little lane at Thorn. Turn right towards Middle Heltor. Just before reaching a house, turn left up another little lane, with an orchard on the right, climbing to reach a gate. Cross the stile in the right-hand field corner (hidden by bushes!) to emerge on to a lane. Turn right and descend into the little settlement of Westcott.

Just before the farmyard follow a yellow waymark rightwards and up to two gates. Go through the one immediately ahead into a little lane. Go over a stile and across the meadow beyond to reach another stile. Go over on to a track between walls and follow it into Westcott Wood. Now keep a little left to emerge, after $^1/_4$ mile, on to the B3212. Turn right, with care, with the wood to your right for a short $^1/_2$ mile, then take a bridleway on the left (marked with a blue paint spot), following it with more woodland on your right. Descend to a stream which sometimes offers quite a muddy crossing and ascend from the other side, first across pasture, then left on an access drive. Leave the drive by turning right before reaching the farm at Leign and, still ascending, go through trees, emerging with a wall to your left. Still climbing and heading northwards, make for some buildings ahead. Keep to the left of these and pick up a similar lane heading westwards on to Mardon Down. Keep just to the right of the high point, continuing to reach, another $^1/_4$ mile on the cross-tracks of Headless Cross.

Turn left along a clear track and the road edge for $^1/_3$ mile then go right to reach the Giant's Grave and ancient cairns at a height of 1171 feet. Continue for $^1/_2$ mile, then turn right along a rough road which winds round to the right and so back towards the Headless Cross.

There now follows a pleasant easy road walk heading downhill for more than a mile, sometimes steeply, and then going through pine trees before crossing the River Teign at Clifford Bridge. Cross the bridge, and continue to Clifford Cross. Here, turn right on the well-signed path back to Steps Bridge. Please do not attempt to walk by the river bank, obeying the National Trust warnings of unstable conditions. Enjoy instead the many delights on offer, not the least of which is the Steps Inn near the end of the journey.

POINTS OF INTEREST:

In autumn the colours of the final $2^1/_2$ miles are a splendid climax to this fine walk, while in spring daffodils and other early flowers abound.

REFRESHMENTS:

The Steps Inn, at the start.

Walk 50   COSDON BEACON AND HOUND TOR   9¹/₂m (15km)
Maps: OS Sheets Landranger 191; Outdoor Leisure 28.
The bare and empty landscape of northern Dartmoor.
Start: At 642941, the Devonshire Inn, Sticklepath.

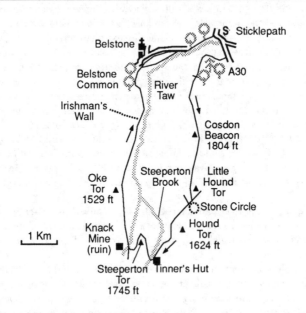

NB. This challenging walk should not be attempted in poor visibility. Even in good weather, a compass, knowledge of its use and a good map are essential.

From the Devonshire Inn in **Sticklepath** (on the A30, 4 miles east of Okehampton), follow the main road, with great care, eastwards across the bridge and then turn right along the river path, heading upstream into a wood. Bear left and ascend, then go right as the ground levels out. Go through a gate and turn sharp left, with a field edge to the left, and continue on to the moor. The way is now almost due south for 1¹/₂ miles making for the rise of Cosdon Beacon ('Cawsand' on some maps). Maintain the southerly course, going gently downhill for a further 1¹/₂ miles, then climbing gently to Little Hound Tor and a stone circle about 250 yards further on. Ignore other tracks hereabouts, bearing right (south-westwards) for a short ¹/₂ mile, then making for the rise of Hound Tor. The track passes to the right of the tor, so a short detour is necessary to visit. Now keep descending to Steeperton Brook and the adjacent old tinner's hut. Continue to a ford, about $\frac{1}{2}$ mile further on.

Cross the brook and turn right, almost due north, climbing to Steeperton Tor. Now go left and downhill, south westwards, to the remains of Knack Mine. Once again cross a stream, and turn right, northwards, heading for the next rise in the landscape almost one mile distant. This is Oke Tor: pass it on the left, with the infant River Taw down in the gorge on the right, and maintain the same northerly direction, the next landmark being the faint line of the Irishman's Wall joining the now stony track from the west another mile on. The route continues towards the edge of the moor, heading for **Belstone** and its welcoming refreshments. An alternative is to strike right, just before the village, to go along the riverside and through attractive Belstone Cleave and Skaigh Wood. The alternative from the Belstone Inn is to walk eastwards back along the lane for $1\frac{1}{2}$ miles to Sticklepath.

POINTS OF INTEREST:

Sticklepath – The village has a very interesting museum housing blacksmithing tools and foundry machinery. To the rear is a Quaker burial ground: many Quakers from the district sailed to the USA with Penn to help found Pennsylvania. Sticklepath means steep path, named after the hill at the western end of the village.

Belstone – A little stone-built village with wood and stone constructed village stocks. The church is very plain and simple with low granite pillars and rough tombstones.

The lonely expanse of north Dartmoor with three tors around 1600 feet and the Taw valley will provide the walker with many opportunities for compass-work and photography.

Bronze Age relics in the area include a burial cairn on Cosdon Beacon, the stone circle near Hound Tor and the White Moor Stone 200 yards south-east – probably a memorial stone.

REFRESHMENTS:

The Devonshire Inn, Sticklepath.
The Belstone Inn, Belstone.

Walk 51　　TWO BRIDGES AND ROUGH TOR　　9¹/₂m (15km)

Maps: OS Sheets Landranger 191; Outdoor Leisure 28.

A long, demanding moorland walk. Clear visibility, map and compass are essential.

Start: At 609751, the car park in the disused quarry, Two Bridges.

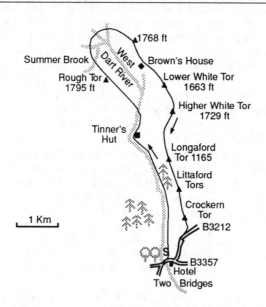

First check that there is no firing on the nearby ranges and then be sure to take compass, map, and some refreshments (both food and drink) before setting off.

Head northwards from the car park, following a clear track, with the West Dart River to your left. Ascend fairly gently for two miles to reach **Wistman's Wood** and the old pillow mounds, to the right. Follow the river, which bends left and right a further mile on, until the prominent Higher White Tor is off to the right, due east, and Rough Tor is clearly seen ahead and a little left. Now cross the river where possible (mud can make this a bit of a problem!) and climb over open moorland to reach Rough Tor and its adjacent firing range notice board.

Maintain the north-north-westerly course for another $1/2$ mile to cross Summer Brook and two more streams. Now bear right in an arc through marshy ground and go over the infant West Dart River. Continue bearing right, eventually heading south-eastwards to the top of the unnamed high point (1795 feet – 539m) to the north-east of Rough Tor.

Now head southwards, descending to the ruins of **Brown's House**. Continue south-eastwards to reach the next objective, the top of Lower White Tor about $1/2$ mile further on. Now turn southwards again to reach Higher White Tor - the distance from Brown's House to this view point being some $1^1/_4$ miles along a ridge offering fine views in all directions.

From Higher White Tor you must now head south-westwards to Longaford Tor, then turn due south once more for two miles of gently descent to **Crockern Tor** and the main road at **Parson's Cottage**. Turn right along the B3212, taking great care as the road can be busy in summer, to return to Two Bridges and the start.

POINTS OF INTEREST:

Wistman's Wood – The OS map shows this as a conifer wood, but there are many stunted oaks and some mountain ash. This area is a very ancient woodland - trees are a rare sight on Dartmoor - with a floor of rushes, ferns and whortleberries (also known as bilberries or blueberries).

Brown's House – The local story concerns a miserable farmer, 'Old Brown' who married a bonny local lass but jealously kept her away from other young attractions by attempting to farm this inhospitable area of the moor, keeping her close at home and always in view. The farm failed, and the home fell into disrepair. What became of the couple is not clear. Later, the ruin was used by local peat cutters and horsemen, its shelter no doubt welcome in bad weather.

Crockern Tor – Tin was mined in the South-West Peninsula from Bronze Age times, the tinners using open-cast methods and, later, horizontal tunnels. In the 12th and 13th centuries tin production was a particularly important industry and evidence can be found all over Cornwall and Devon. Gradually the workmen evolved a system of self-government with special local laws, coinage and taxes. The 'parliament' (or Great Court) for this self-government was, at one time, held on Crockern Tor. There was a Stannary Prison in Lydford.

Parson's Cottage – The cottage is so-called because the Vicar of Widecombe, the Reverend Mason, built a house here in the last century.

REFRESHMENTS:

None on the route, so please go prepared. There is a hotel in Two Bridges.

Walk 52   SHIPLEY BRIDGE AND RED LAKE   10m (16km)

Maps: OS Sheets Landranger 202; Outdoor Leisure 28.

A fine long Dartmoor walk. Clear conditions and map and compass required.

Start: At 681629, Shipley Bridge car park, near Didsworthy.

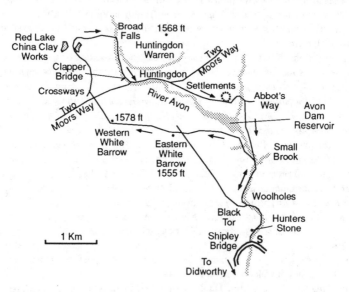

This demanding walk across the southern part of the Dartmoor National Park should not be attempted in mist. In good weather the walker will be well rewarded with fine views, many relics of ancient man and evidence of Devon's more recent industrial past. The walk begins at the popular-in-summer car park at Shipley Bridge, about 3 miles north of South Brent and $^3/_4$ mile north of Didsworthy.

Walk northwards from the car park along the banks of the River Avon, passing the Hunter's Stone and the one-time Youth Hostel. The route crosses and recrosses the river until, about $1^1/_2$ miles from the start, the track steepens as it approaches the western end of the Avon Dam Reservoir's dam. At the dam, strike due westward across the open moorland for a further mile, aiming for Eastern White Barrow - a Bronze Age burial mound and a **1240 Perambulation Point**.

The route now continues north-westwards for another mile to reach Western White Barrow and its cairn, hut and Sir William Petre's boundary cross. A few yards further on, a trench is reached. In this a tramway once ran, transporting of peat cut from the moor down to Shipley. Follow this trench northwards to Crossways. The Two Moors Way crosses here, heading roughly east-west. Our walk does not follow the Way, following the clear mineral railway track northwards to reach the spoil mound and flooded tips of Red Lake **China Clay** works.

Now turn right, due east, for $^1/_2$ mile to reach Broad Falls on the infant River Avon. Cross the river and turn south, passing **Pillow Mounds** and the remains of tin mines to reach a little clapper bridge. Here, the route turns left (heading eastwards again), following The Two Moors Way to reach Huntingdon Cross. Continue for another mile, heading east-south-eastwards, passing ancient hut circles and settlements and with the Reservoir off to the right. Cross the (sometimes boggy) Western Wella Brook, then turn right to follow a track down to the eastern end of the Reservoir's dam. Continue for a further $^3/_4$ mile to rejoin the outward route near Small Brook. Now retrace your steps back to the start.

POINTS OF INTEREST:

1240 Perambulation Point – In 1240 twelve knights rode around some thirty tors, stones or other landmarks to set the boundary of the Forest of Dartmoor. This point was one of the markers on this difficult journey.

China Clay – This essential ingredient of fine porcelain was extracted here from 1910 until 1932 and taken south to the drying-works at Bittaford via the mineral railway.

Pillow Mounds – These are, or were, man-made warrens when rabbits were extensively reared on Dartmoor for fur and table.

REFRESHMENTS:

None en route, although an ice-cream van sometimes parks at Shipley Bridge. Walkers must therefore take their own, or visit nearby South Brent which has both inns and stores.

Walk 53　　NORTH-EAST DARTMOOR　　10½m (17km)

Maps: OS Sheets Landranger 191; Outdoor Leisure 28.

A long and challenging moorland walk requiring good visibility, careful map reading and a compass.

Start: At 659839, Fernworthy Reservoir.

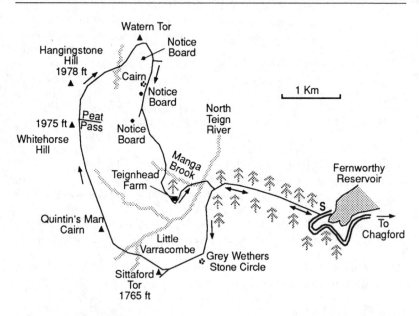

The start is some 3 miles west of Chagford, at the western end of Fernworthy Reservoir.

Begin by walking westward through the dark coniferous forest for a mile, ascending to a gate and going through to emerge on to the open moor. Turn left, southwards, with the forest's edge to your left. Cross a wall and maintain the southerly direction to reach a second wall. Cross this to reach the **Grey Wethers Stone Circle**.

Now turn right, west-south-westwards, aiming for Sittaford Tor (1,765 feet – 538m) just ½ mile away, the top of which offers good views to the south and east. From the Tor, follow the wall that runs north-westwards, descending into the sometimes boggy head-waters of the River Teign and then climbing up to the cairn of Quintin's Man. The walk continues north-westwards along a ridge heading for

Whitehorse Hill and the **Peat Pass** and then swinging north-eastwards to descend into Watern Combe, which can be boggy after rain. From the Combe, climb up to Watern Tor (1726 feet – 526m). The oddly shaped layers of granite here are the result of prehistoric 'layering' and centuries of wind, ice and frost. At the northern end of the Tor is a 'thirlstone', a rock with a 'thirle' or hole, the ancient name being the same as at Thurlestone – on the coast to the south, and also featured in one of the walk's in this book – where the hole is an arched stone off-shore.

Continue this walk by turning right, south-south-eastwards, towards a wall-corner. Follow the wall southwards, passing a cairn and a firing-range notice board, to the right. After $^1/_2$ mile, turn a little to the left to descend to Manga Brook. Cross the Brook and continue to the ruin of Teignhead Farm with its clump of evergreens. Now turn north-eastwards to reach a clapper bridge, crossing and then continuing to reach to the forest gate passed through earlier in the walk. From the gate, retrace your footsteps through the forest to return to the start.

POINTS OF INTEREST:

Grey Wethers Stone Circle – Another Dartmoor circle of stones dating back to the Bronze Age. This circle appears, to some, to resemble a group of sheep – hence the name, a wether being the local word for a castrated ram.

Peat Pass – As in many parts of Dartmoor this area of the moor produced a good peat for fuel. Peat passes were (and still are) tracks – often in deep gullies – cut to help the peat cutters, farmers, sheep and cattle (and now walkers) reach other parts of the moor.

REFRESHMENTS:

Nothing en route, so you will need to take your own. The nearest hostelry is the *Bullers Arms* in Chagford.

Walk 54   FUR TOR AND TAVY CLEAVE   10¹/₂m (17km)

Maps: OS Sheets Landranger 191; Outdoor Leisure 28.

A long, strenuous walk with damp bits, rough walking and a deep gorge. Map, compass and a clear day required.

Start: At 537802, Wapsworthy.

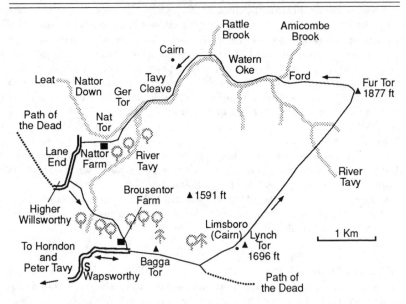

If there is insufficient parking in the hamlet of Wapsworthy, an alternative start might be found at the end of the lane near Brousentor Farm (at 546805) or at Lanehead (at 536824). Small adjustments to the route will then be necessary. Check the firing details on the Dartmoor ranges and the weather forecast before setting out on this walk.

From Wapsworthy follow the road northwards and then eastwards to reach a T-junction at one of the alternative starts (546805). To the left, the track leads to Brousentor Farm but the walk continues eastwards with Bagga Tor off to the left. This is part of **The Path of the Dead**: both Coffin Wood and Corpse Lane are nearby! After about a mile, as the walls either side widen and ultimately swing north and south, walk north-eastwards, aiming for Limsboro Cairn and Lynch Tor about ³/₄ mile further on. The cairn here is another 1240 Perambulation Point (*see* Note to Walk 52).

Maintain direction (north-eastwards) for two more miles, crossing first the infant River Tavy and then a smaller brook. Now go steeply uphill for another mile to reach the remote top of Fur Tor, a fine view point and claimed to be the point of inaccessibility of Dartmoor. This is tough walking country and the next stage, heading due west and downhill, requires determination too. The target is a mile away, where the Amicombe Brook meets the Tavy at Sandy Ford. At Sandy Ford, cross to the north side of the Tavy, skirting Watern Oke, and follow the river as it bends north-westwards. Next, cross the Rattle Brook and swing south-westwards to enter the steep gorge of Tavy Cleave. The Cleave is almost two miles of unusual scenery for Dartmoor, an enclosed, narrow valley rather then open country. Leave the River Tavy at an old Leat which has come down from Nattor Down, and contour below the tors of Ger and Nat to gain the track leading past Nattor Farm to reach a lane at the aptly named Lane End.

Turn left down the lane going through several gates to reach, after ¹/₂ mile, just before the lane bends off to the right, the Path of the Dead (again) at Higher Willsworthy. Turn left on to the deep and rocky track. After about 250 yards, go over a stile on the right, marked by a signpost and head south to a field corner. Now follow yellow waymarks alongside four fields, dropping down all the while, to reach the River Tavy again by some trees. Cross the 'dodgy' stepping-stones (!), with great care, and go eastwards and then south-eastwards, following more, and clearer waymarkers. Go past Brousentor Farm (right) and continue to reach the T-junction at the alternative start at 546805. Now retrace the outward route along the lane to the right to return to Wapsworthy.

POINTS OF INTEREST:

The Path of the Dead – This path leads from the old farms around Postbridge and Bellever to Lydford. Corpses for burial in Lydford were taken across the moor in canvas sacks slung over the backs of horses. On reaching Brousentor or Coffin Wood the bodies were decently transferred to coffins for the final miles to St Petroc's Church in Lydford. If the weather was so severe that graves could not be dug in the hard ground, it was not unknown for corpses to be salted down and stored to await improved digging conditions!

REFRESHMENTS:

None en route but nearby are:
The Castle Inn, Lydford.
The Elephant Inn, Horndon.
The Peter Tavy Inn, Peter Tavy.

Walk 55   CORN RIDGE AND GREAT LINKS TOR   11m (17$\frac{1}{2}$km)
Maps: OS Sheets Landranger 191; Outdoor Leisure 28.
A long, lonely adventure across bare moorland, compass and map essential.
Start: At 523853, The Dartmoor Inn, Lydford.

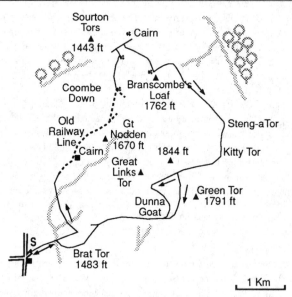

A wild landscape with, given the right visibility, superb views make this walk a 'special' – but do go well equipped and prepared.

    Leave the inn, at a crossroads on the A388 near Lydford, south-west of Okehampton, by heading north-eastwards along a bridleway towards open moor. Cross a ford after $\frac{1}{2}$ mile and follow the bridleway uphill for a further $\frac{1}{4}$ mile. Now when the bridleway swings right towards Brat Tor, turn left and cross a brook. After another $\frac{1}{4}$ mile, cross the infant River Lyd at a second ford. Now turn half-right, north-north-eastwards, to follow an **Old Railway Line**, passing Great Nodden, to the right, to reach the loop on Corn Ridge. The steep valley leading to Tor Wood and the crags of Sourton Tors are off to the left as the route turns right for 400 yards or so, then heads south-westwards, uphill, towards the lonely rock and an ancient cairn at the top of

Branscombe's Loaf. The route now continues on the lower contour, curving right as it avoids boggy ground, to the right, and the steep valley of **Black-a-Tor Copse** below and to the left.

After about $1^1/_4$ miles, at Steng-a-Tor, bear right again, heading due south, for $^1/_3$ mile (it can be boggy!) to reach Kitty Tor and a firing-range notice board. Now turn westward away from the Danger Area, and continue down to the desolate ruins of an old peat works. Maintain the west-south-westward direction and climb up to Great Links Tor. Pass the tall granite pillar and turn right for the western end of the stone piles, at 1923 feet (586m). After enjoying the views to the south and east, turn south-east to reach the two granite outcrops at Dunna Goat. Now follow the bridleway heading due west, following it for a long mile and passing old tin workings, to the left. Beyond these, bear half-left to reach Brat Tor and then go west to **Widgery Cross**. To complete the walk, bear a little left, then gently right down to the ford passed on the outward route. Now reverse the outward route back to the Dartmoor Inn.

POINTS OF INTEREST:
The Old Railway Line – The line was constructed in 1879 to transport peat cut from the moor to the main line of the London and South West Railway near Bridestow.
Branscombe's Loaf – The name derives from a story that, in the 13th century, Bishop Branscombe met a strange rider on the moor who offered to give him bread and cheese if the Bishop doffed his cap and called him 'Master'. The Bishop was just about to do this when his servant noticed the rider's cloven hoofs. The Bishop made the sign of the cross and the stranger vanished, leaving the bread and cheese turned to stone.
Black-a-Tor Copse – This oak tree woodland is unusually high up on the windswept moor.
Widgery Cross – The painter, William Widgery, erected this great stone cross to commemorate the Golden Jubilee of Queen Victoria in 1887.

REFRESHMENTS:
The Dartmoor Inn, Lydford.

Walk 56   BOLT HEAD AND BOLT TAIL   11m (17½km)

Maps: OS Sheets Landranger 202; Outdoor Leisure 20.

Pleasant inland countryside and miles of splendid cliff walking.

Start: At 730381, the South Sands car park, Salcombe.

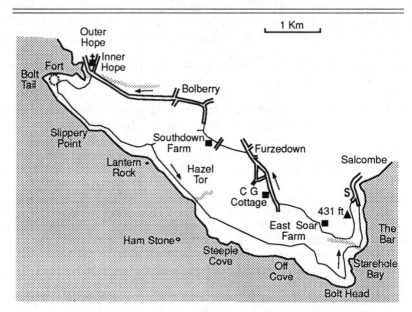

From the car park, to the south of **Salcombe**, walk pass the main entrance of **Overbeck Gardens**, to the left, and continue through the palm trees (!) Go past the National Trust cairn to reach a signpost indicating 'Sharp Tor and Upper Cliff Path'. Go past the trig. point, to the right, and pause at the viewpoint of Sharp Tor.

At the path junction just ahead, follow the sign for 'Soar Mill Cove', going over a stile and across a field to reach the next signpost. Keeping this to your left, walk ahead, passing East Soar Farm, to your right. Now cross another stile and follow the yellow waymarks to reach a lane and car park. Turn right along the lane, going past the old coastguard cottages. At a junction do not go left: instead, go straight on, maintaining the north-westward course. Soon the lane is joined by another from the left: keep straight ahead for a few yards, then go left along a footpath, heading slightly north of west and going through Southdown Farm. Now continue across fields, heading north-westwards, for a short $\frac{1}{4}$ mile to reach a lane. Follow this northwards to reach its T-junction with a lane. Turn left to reach Bolberry, going through the hamlet and then following a lane that descends into **Hope Cove**.

Inner and Outer Hope are worth exploring, and welcome refreshments are available before continuing along the route. To continue, walk south and then take the South West Coastal Path, signed 'Bolt Tail $\frac{1}{2}$ mile', passing the Old Lifeboat Station. Go right, up some steps, and through a kissing-gate. Now follow the Path's waymarks around the headland (beware of crumbly cliffs and keep dogs on leads) and the ancient fort, continuing south-eastwards for 4 miles or so of grand walking. Ignore all paths going inland and, in due course, the Path will lead you to a kissing-gate leading to Bolt Head above the Mew Stones and Starehole Cove. This is another place to rest and explore, with opportunities for bird and butterfly watching and camerawork). Now drop down on to the lower path, signed 'Sharp Tor and Overbeck', and follow the 'Courtenay Walk' for a mile through woodland, with fine views across The Bar and Salcombe Harbour. When a road junction is reached, keep right to return to the car park.

POINTS OF INTEREST:

Salcombe – A fine resort on the Kingsbridge Estuary with attractive shops, old cottages and a good local history museum, with an especially interesting section on the US forces stationed hereabouts during World War II.

Overbeck Gardens – This beautiful 6 acre garden, which has many rare plants and shrubs, is a National Trust property, open daily from April to October. The site's elegant Edwardian house is now a museum, with a fine collection of old local photographs and equally interesting collections of shells, model boats, birds and animals.

Hope Cove – Our early ancestors populated the Iron Age Fort on the headland of Bolt Tail. At the Cove are the remains of a jetty said to have been built by the Danes. Hope has been used for centuries as a much needed shelter by ships escaping wild storms raging along the Channel and there was once a very thriving pilchard and mackerel fleet based here.

REFRESHMENTS:

There is a very wide variety of choices in Salcombe, and a good selection at Hope Cove.

Walk 57   LYDFORD'S FOREST AND GORGE   11m (17¹/₂km)

Maps: OS Sheets Landranger 191; Pathfinder 1327.

A long, but splendid, walk through farmland, forest and a spectacular gorge (admission fee, dogs on leads).

Start: At 513852, the War Memorial, Lydford.

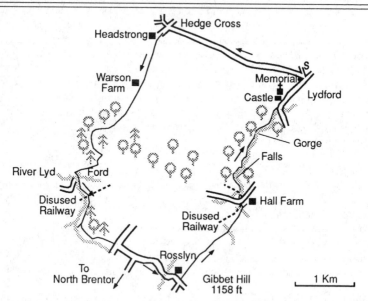

From the War Memorial, at the northern end of **Lydford**, take the lane signed to Coryton for 1¹/₂ miles to reach Hedge Cross. Turn left along a lane for 100 yards to reach the buildings at Headstrong, then fork left along the access track to Warson Farm. Just before the farm buildings, follow yellow footpath signs, going left and then right (this section may be muddy), but maintaining the same general direction as you go through gates to reach pasture. Now with a deep, forested valley down to your left, keep up to the right, ascending beside a hedge, to the right, to reach a gate into a wood. The track beyond gradually descends through the trees, and after ¹/₃ mile emerges into an open area, with a field to the left. The track heads back into the trees for a short distance, then swings left, southwards: follow more yellow arrows as you plunge into a steep, rocky, narrow cleft for a further ¹/₃ mile. Care is required on this section in slippery conditions.

At the bottom, bear right, then follow yet more yellow arrows to go, firstly, left, then right to reach a stile. Go over, emerging from the woodland into a field. Walk diagonally across the field (south-westwards) to reach a gate on to a lane. Turn right, but soon follow left, descending to a footbridge and ford at the River Lyd. Now do not follow the road on the right: instead, walk ahead, ascending (and ignoring tracks to the left) along the river valley. Pass immediately to the left of a house and continue uphill into a conifer wood. On reaching a broad crossing track, turn right and, shortly after going through a gate, go around to the left. Go under a bridge (there used to be a railway above) and, as the broad track bends off to the right, fork half-left, uphill, with a little tributary of the Lyd rushing far below. Climb steadily up, with the stream down to the right, to reach a gate at the top. Go through and walk alongside the hedge on the right to reach a second gate about 50 yards further on. Now go diagonally right, across rough pasture, then down and up to reach a third gate. Go through and keep alongside the hedge on the left for two fields to reach a road. Go straight over and follow the lane opposite. Ignore a lane to the right, leading to North Brentor, continuing to cross the River Burn. Now, just short of Rosslyn Cottage, keep right to reach the open moor below Gibbet Hill. Turn left along the clear track running north-eastwards, following it for a mile and crossing two shallow streams to reach a gate on the left, before Hall Farm. Go through, cross a bridge (over the old railway) and continue to a road. Follow the sign for **Lydford Gorge** and, paying the appropriate fee and perhaps pausing for refreshments, descend along well-marked paths to the beautiful White Lady waterfall.

Now follow the path alongside the river, off to the right, heading northwards for more than a mile. Before leaving the Gorge, follow the signs to view the Devil's Cauldron before climbing out to the exit, on the right, and the main road. Turn left and ascend steeply back into Lydford, passing the Castle, to the left. Finally, walk through this old Saxon settlement to regain the start.

POINTS OF INTEREST:

Lydford – The Castle was a prison rather than a 'real' castle. Be sure to find the epitaph to George Routleigh, a watch and clockmaker in St Petroc's churchyard.
Lydford Gorge – A magnificent gorge, cut by the River Lyd. The White Lady waterfall is named for the ghost of a maiden which, if seen, will protect the viewer from drowning. The Devil's Cauldron is a series of pot holes worn smooth by the river.

REFRESHMENTS:
The Castle Inn, Lydford.
Also available at the National Trust's entrances to Lydford Gorge.

Walk 58   COUNTISBURY AND COUNTY GATE $11^1/_2$m (18km)

Maps: OS Sheets Landranger 180; Outdoor Leisure 9.

A long, strenuous walk through a fine wooded valley and along part of the South West Coastal Path.

Start: At 753496, Countisbury car park.

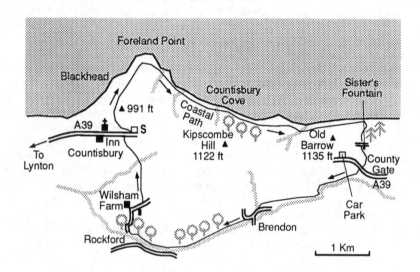

This demanding, but most rewarding walk in the north-eastern corner of Devon, begins at the Countisbury car park. The car park lies on the seaward side of the A39 at the top of Countisbury Hill, about 3 miles east of Lynmouth.

Take the path heading westward from the back of the car park, going alongside the wall to reach **Countisbury Church**. Now follow the signed 'Coast Path to Lighthouse', turning right after $^1/_2$ mile to visit the Foreland Lighthouse (which, ultimately, involves a short detour to the left) and then continuing along a short stretch of road, to the right. When the road turns right and inland, turn left with the Coastal Path for a splendid $1^1/_2$ miles of dramatic cliff scenery, with plenty of ups and downs, and occasional waymarks. On reaching a combe near the high point of Old Barrow Hill, follow a path heading inland and then back to the coast. After another mile of eastward walking, turn right along a path signed 'Culbone'. Go right through a gateway, then left to reach **'Sister's Fountain'**. Now ascend, and then go right along a track signed for, and leading to, **County Gate**.

Cross the A39, with care, to reach a car park. Now take the middle of three paths, signed 'Brendon', heading south-westwards. After $^1/_2$ mile you will reach a gate: obey the orange waymarkers, descending to cross a footbridge. Go down steps and continue along a field path to into the valley of the East Lyn River. When you reach a road, bear right into the village of **Brendon**. Now ignore the left turn over a bridge (unless refreshments are required, in which case an inn is handy - return to this junction to continue the walk) continuing along the road for 120 yards and then taking the track ahead as the road bends right. There now follows a $1^1/_4$ miles stretch of fine, wooded valley walking, along the riverside. When a bridge is reached, turn left into the hamlet of **Rockford** to reach an inn, returning here for the final leg of the walk.

Now bear right and ascend for 100 yards, following a path signed 'Countisbury via Wilsham'. After a further $^1/_4$ mile, go right, then left between walls and left once again to reach an old farmhouse. The track turns right to pass to the left of the new Wilsham Farmhouse, then continues to reach a double gate. Go through the left-hand gate and continue northwards, downhill into a valley – following the yellow waymarkers. Go over a stream and climb up to reach the A39. Turn right, with care, then cross, again with care, to reach the car park.

POINTS OF INTEREST:

Countisbury Church – The church is notable for its fine 18th-century rood screen.
Sister's Fountain – The cross marks the spot where Joseph of Arimathea is supposed to have rested before continuing his journey to Glastonbury. The top of Old Barrow Hill nearby is the site of a Roman fort and signalling station.
County Gate – Exactly on the border of Somerset and Devon, the site has an information centre, toilets and, sometimes, an ice cream van.
Brendon – St Brendon's Church has a interesting sundial, dated 1707, over the porch.
Rockford – Local crafts are to be found on sale opposite the inn.

REFRESHMENTS:

The Sandpiper, Countisbury, at the top Countisbury Hill.
The Inn, Brendon.
The Rockford Inn, Rockford.

Walk 59 GOLITHA FALLS AND SIBLYBACK RESERVOIR 3m (5km)
Maps: OS Sheets Landranger 201; Pathfinder 1348.
An easy walk visiting two 'beauty spots' on Bodmin Moor.
Start: At 227690, the car park north-west of St Cleer.

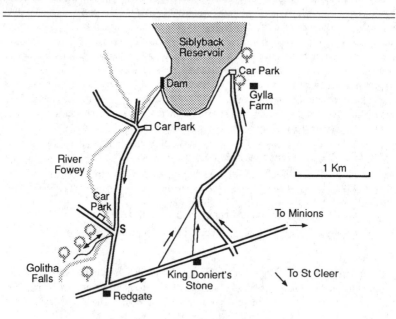

This easy walk commences at a car park about 5 miles north of Liskeard, near the **Golitha Falls**, River Fowey.

From the car park, follow the river southwards for a short $\frac{1}{2}$ mile, going through beech woods to reach the falls. The water cascades and sparkles following rain, and if the sun shines the walker will be reluctant to return to the car park to continue the walk, but needs so to do!

On returning, turn right, cross the river and go right again, following the road to a junction. Turn left to visit the **King Doniert Stone**. The traffic on this road may well be quite heavy on summer weekends, so care is required. The road walking can be shortened by not visiting the stone, but forking left along a footpath before it is reached. The route from the stone takes the footpath directly opposite, heading north across the scrub and moor towards some buildings. This route reaches the first footpath near

118

where a road is joined. The simplest route (the third variation!) is to continue along the road towards Minions for 300 yards or so beyond the stone and then to turn left, following the lane through a little hamlet. This lane is the one reached by the two footpaths and is followed northwards to the **Siblyback Lake** – a reservoir – where there is another car park.

To return to the start, turn left and walk alongside the southern lake shore to reach the dam. Now turn left to a third car parking area. Follow the road from there, heading southwards for $\frac{1}{2}$ mile to reach the start point.

POINTS OF INTEREST:

Golitha Falls – The beautiful falls entice picnickers and gentle strollers on most weekends.

King Doniert's Stone – This is a well-preserved monument – probably 9th-century – to King Doniert (?King of Cornwall and also known as Durngarth) – with an inscription *Doniert Rogavit Pro Anima* – 'Doniert prayed for his soul', and a clear pattern of interlacing.

Siblyback Reservoir – A pleasant little valley was flooded to provide a reservoir of drinking water, but the resulting lake has also provided an opportunity for canoeists, yachtsmen and anglers to enjoy their sport.

REFRESHMENTS:

Nothing on the route, but there is an inn at St Cleer, 1 mile south-east of the King's Stone, and, in summer, the occasional ice cream van at the car park(s).

Also nearby is the Cheesewring Inn, Minions.

Walk 60   **BOSCASTLE HARBOUR AND VALLEY**   3m (5km)

Maps: OS Sheets Landranger 190; Explorer 9.

An easy, gentle walk beside the harbour and along the delightful valley of the River Valency.

Start: At 100913, Boscastle's main car park.

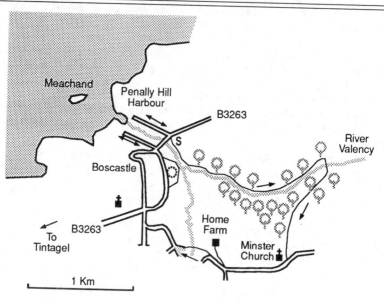

Be sure to have a camera to photograph the unique sheltered harbour of **Boscastle** and the many other features that this short but attractive walk offers.

Begin by leaving the rear of the town's main car park and going left along a footpath which leads to the bank of the River Valency. Walk beside the river, with the water always close on your right – the going can be muddy after rain – for almost $1\frac{1}{2}$ miles. On reaching a footbridge, cross and ascend through woodland. The path turns left after a short distance and soon reaches a road at Minster Church.

Turn right along the road, continuing straight on where the access track to Home Farm goes off right and another lane bends left. Now, after another 250 yards or so, the road swings left: cross a stile on the right and bear left across the field beyond to reach another lane. Follow the lane to a road. Turn right towards Boscastle, but soon turn right again along a signed footpath leading to Bottreaux castle. This can be identified merely by a mound in the field.

Turn left to rejoin the road in the village and, before returning to the start, explore the harbour, wandering each side and, perhaps, climbing above to the cliffs which offer fine opportunities for photography. There is also an excellent museum near the car park as well as many pretty houses and narrow streets.

POINTS OF INTEREST:
Boscastle – The little village was once an important harbour not just as a refuge in stormy weather but as a port for importing coal and limestone, and for exporting grain, slate and manganese ore. A floating mine accidentally blew up the outer breakwater during the 1939 - 45 War but this has been rebuilt by the National Trust who also own the nearby cliffs and headlands.

REFRESHMENTS:
There are inns, cafés and restaurants in Boscastle to cater for all tastes.

Walks 61 & 62   GWENNAP AND PORTHCURNO   3½m (6km)
or 6½m (10km)

Maps: OS Sheets Landranger 203; Explorer 7.
The South West Coastal Path and inland farmland, with many ascents and descents.
Start: At 381222, St Levan Church, south of the B3215.

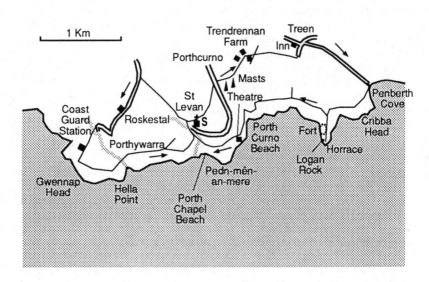

From **St Levan's Church**, leave the churchyard at the north-east corner and walk via stone stiles to pass to the left of Rospletha. Now go along the clear track to **Porthcurno**. On reaching the road, cross straight over, keeping some garages off to the right. At the Communications College, take the signed footpath on the left and maintain the north-easterly direction to pass the aerials. Continue to reach Trendrennen Farm. Go through the buildings and then bear left and right over a stone stile. Now walk forwards across several fields, linked by stiles, heading more easterly to reach the road at Treen. Turn left, passing the inn, and at the junction turn right to follow the lane which descends to Penberth Cove. By the stone slipway, look for the Coastal Path sign to the right and follow the Path, ascending to Cribba Head. Follow the cliff path for

$1^1/_2$ miles of wonderful scenery, heading westwards and passing the Iron Age fort at Treryn Dinas and the **Logan Rock** (which requires a short diversion southwards). Continue along the well-signed Coastal Path, reaching Porthcurno Beach, then taking one of the alternative routes either above or below the famous **Minack Theatre**. The easier way is to the right, going through the car park. Continue to the fine headland of Pedn-men-an-Mere from where the route regains St Levan's Church by taking the right-hand path above Porth Chapel Beach.

The shorter walk ends at the church, but the longer route continues to the road end. From there, maintain direction, going uphill and passing a cottage to reach a stone stile. Go over into a field and follow its left-edge to reach a second stile. Go over and walk up the right edge of the next field to reach a third stile. Go over and head north-westwards, crossing five more fields (linked by stiles) to reach a road. Turn left, southwards, and follow the road into Roskestal. Follow the road through the hamlet, continuing for about 250 yards to where the road turns sharp left. There, turn right along a track. The track soon turns southwards: stay with it, crossing a stream and continuing to the Coast Guard Station. Now do not turn right to follow paths down to Porth Loe: instead, turn left on to the South West Coastal Path, following it around Gwennap Head and down to Porthgwarra. Now turn right at a signpost and ascend to pass a house. Go right once more, following the cliff path down to the beach at Porth Chapel to join the shorter route again, or go half-left and inland to return to St Levan's Church.

POINTS OF INTEREST:

St Levan's Church – Well worth an exploration: its bench-ends, rood screen and Norman font are but three items of note.

Porthcurno – With its shell-beach, is where many submarine communication cables come ashore.

The Logan Rock – Logan rocks are perched boulders which rock gently when pushed. Legend has it that the rocking foretells the future to those who can 'read' the movement. This logan, weighing more than 65 tons, once balanced on Treryn Dinas, but a young naval officer and some crew members dislodged it in 1824. The officer was made to replace it some six months later, but it has not rocked properly since the incident.

Minack Theatre – Opened in 1932, the theatre was carved to form a 'natural' amphitheatre. Many dramatic productions are held on summer evenings, with a magnificent backdrop of sky and sea.

REFRESHMENTS:
The Logan Rock, Treen.

Walk 63   ST EWE AND POLMASSICK   4m (6½km)

Maps: OS Sheets Landranger 204; Pathfinder 1361.

Quiet country lanes in south Cornwall, near Mevagissey.

Start: At 977461, St Ewe Church.

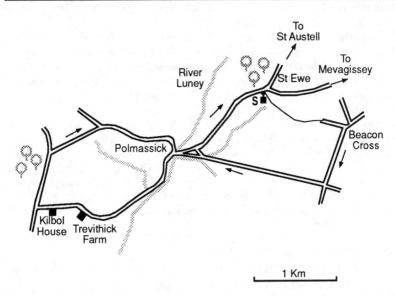

From the church in the tiny village of St Ewe – set on a secondary road 5 miles west of Mevagissey – take the path running south-east from the left corner of the churchyard and follow it down to a stream. This path may well be soggy and overgrown, but it soon improves as it ascends towards farm buildings. Go through two gates and then turn left through the farm, going along the farm access road to reach a lane at Beacon Cross. Turn right and follow the lane to the next crossroads. Turn right again, going along a very narrow lane – that the locals call Drunkards Lane! – that heads downhill into the hamlet of Polmassick.

Cross the bridge over the River Luney and turn left to follow the lane past – or call in at – the Vineyard. Now follow the lane for a mile as it ascends (heading westwards), passing Trevithick Farm and Kilbol House. Look out for viewpoints between the hedges and a gateway, to the left: the view down to the coast are splendid.

124

When the lane reaches a junction, turn right and walk north for $\frac{1}{4}$ mile to reach a fork. Take the right branch, following the lane for a short $\frac{1}{2}$ mile to reach another junction. Here, go right again, heading downhill back into Polmassick. On this lane, keep a look out, to the left, for deer.

Walk through the hamlet again and then bear left, uphill, to return to St Ewe and the start.

POINTS OF INTEREST:
This walk, given good weather, is full of natural interest, roadside flowers, charming views, no petrol fumes (unless you are unlucky!) and a chance to sample a Cornish wine. You will hear birds and have a quiet and peaceful afternoon – and may even see deer.

REFRESHMENTS:
The Crown Inn, St Ewe.

Walks 64 & 65 LUXULYAN VALLEY AND THE SAINTS WAY 4m (6½ km) or 12m (19km)

Maps: OS Sheets Landranger 200; Pathfinder 1354 and 1347.
A long easy walk with shorter alternative, woods and/or fields.
Start: At 052582, Luxulyan Church.

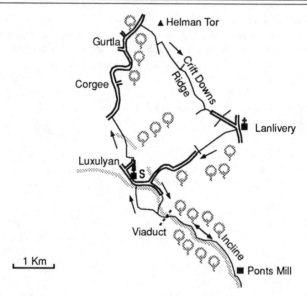

The short walk starts from the granite church of St Cyriac and St Julitta in **Luxulyan** and proceeds eastwards, downhill, for about 400 yards to reach a road fork. Take the right branch, following a leat which runs first on the right then on the left. After a further ½ mile, at the next junction, turn left and immediately right, going between granite posts and into woodland. Go half-left, uphill, and soon follow a footpath, running alongside the leat again, for a fine leafy mile, going under Treffry Viaduct and continuing to reach the ruins of a great water-mill, to the left. About 100 yards beyond, follow the Carmears incline down going under a stone bridge and continuing south, and then south-east, to reach Ponts Mill. Turn about and retrace the route to the spot where the leat discharges by the water wheel. Here, fork left to follow the leat, beside the disused railway (rails and chair still remain in places), back to the

126

Viaduct. Now follow the railway for another 200 yards, going over a smaller viaduct. After a further 100 yards, just before the line crosses a river, turn left along a clear path, descending to steps. On reaching an old shed, fork right and continue alongside the river to reach a stile. Cross and, after another 50 yards, climb the steps over the wall to the left, and go along the right edge of a field. Maintain the northerly course across several more fields, making for Luxulyan Church dead ahead. Cross the old railway once again and so return to Luxulyan Church.

The longer walk now goes north, out of the village, then follows the clearly waymarked 'Saints Way' path uphill. Follow the path through fields and then down into a sometimes muddy valley, using granite stiles to cross stone walls. Cross a little stream and then climb to reach a farm access road, with the farm itself to the right. Go north along the access road to reach a lane. Turn right and walk through the hamlets of Corgee and Gurtla, following Saints Way markers to reach the wooded area of Lowertown. The Saints Way-markers eventually lead you to a right turn. Take this, heading south-eastwards to Helman Tor, which, at 686 feet (209m) affords good views. Maintain the southerly direction along Crift Downs Ridge for a mile to reach a minor road and **Lanlivery**. The route back to the start is almost due west from the village inn, going across fields to reach a lane which leads downhill at first, then uphill into Luxulyan.

POINTS OF INTEREST:

Luxulyan – The granite in this area predominates in the buildings – churches, homes, stiles are all made of it. The same granite was supplied to kerb much of London's streets. Treffry's viaduct spans the valley and makes a dramatic contrast: man's industrial ingenuity and Nature's beauty. It, too, is made of granite. It once carried a railway above a canal and so is, strictly, a via-aqua-duct! The whole enabled granite to be transported from the local quarries to Par and Newquay. The rare tourmaline granite supplied the material for the Duke of Wellington's sarcophagus in St Paul's Cathedral in 1852.

Lanlivery – The church spire is 97 feet tall and the font is large enough for total immersion.

REFRESHMENTS:

Both Luxulyan and Lanlivery have inns which provide good food and drink.

Walk 66   Tintagel   4m (6½km)

Maps: OS Sheets Landranger 200; Pathfinder 1325.

An easy walk with stiles, encompassing legend, ruins and bronze-age carvings.

Start: At 056884, the Old Post Office, Tintagel.

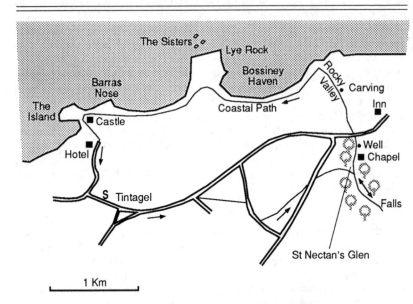

From the Old Post Office (a National Trust property) in **Tintagel** walk uphill, eastwards, and after passing three roads off to the right, cross a stile, also on the right, and bear half-left. Cross three fields, going over stone stiles between them, maintaining direction to reach a lane. Turn right along the lane, following it to reach some buildings, on the left. Go between the first and second houses and cross the stile ahead. Now, with a hedge to the left, cross a field to reach another stile. Go over on to a lane. Turn left and follow the lane for about 200 yards to a point where it bends left. Here turn right over a stile and walk diagonally across the field beyond, descending to reach a stile. Go over into woodland. Continue downhill to reach a bridge over a stream. Cross and go right to reach the café and waterfall of St Nectan's glen. To view the falls a small admission charge is payable.

To continue, retrace your way along the path, passing the bridge and continuing north-westwards, towards the sea, with the stream on your left. A lane is soon reached: follow it to **St Piran's Chapel** and Well. Now go left, and then left again to reach the main road (the B3263). Turn left and follow the road, with care. Cross the stream at Rocky Valley and then turn right along a drive. Go past a café and over a bridge – the **carvings** are signposted here. The carvings are on the rock face at the back of the ruined mill building near the trout farm. After viewing them, continue along the path to reach the seashore at Bossiney Haven. This is a place to linger before turning left on to the Coastal Path. Follow the Path above The Sisters and Barras Nose for about $1^1/_2$ miles, then, on approaching the hotel on the cliff top, go along a path leading to a road to the left of the buildings. Turn left along the road to return to Tintagel.

POINTS OF INTEREST:

Tintagel – Reputed to be King Arthur's birthplace and the meeting place of the Knights of the Round Table. There are the ruins of an ancient monastery, a mineral museum and the Post Office, a small manor house built in the 14th century.

Within the village there is a delightful stream-side walk, gulls and other sea birds wheeling overhead, an abundance of cafés and an inn or two – plus any amount of 'Cornish mementos' on sale.

St Piran's Chapel – The Chapel has a pre-Norman lamp, an ancient stained-glass window. Nearby, there is a Roman milestone.

Carvings – One theory is that these are Bronze-age carvings representing magic mazes. More likely is the theory that they were carved by bored mill workers.

REFRESHMENTS:

There is a wide selection in Tintagel.

Walk 67   PRUSSIA AND PERRANUTHNOE   4m (6½km)

Maps: OS Sheets Landranger 203, Explorer 7.
A short walk along Cornish cliffs and field paths.
Start: At 554283, the car park near Prussia Cove.

This is another of those short walks which might take quite a long time as there are so many places 'just to stand and stare'. Bird watchers and photographers are well-catered for. To reach the start, take the secondary road which runs south from the A394 (signposted for Prussia Cove), going through Rosudgeon and continuing for about ½ mile to reach the car park, to the right.

From the car park, continue eastwards, going right, left and right again as you head downhill to reach Bessy's Cove. Turn right along the acorn-marked South West Coastal Path which leads westwards from **Prussia Cove**, passing **Cudden Point** and going along Stackhouse Cliffs. From here there are fine views across Mounts Bay to **St Michael's Mount** itself, about 3 miles ahead. Two miles from Cudden Point the path descends to Perran Sands. From here refreshments can be sought in the little town before returning to the beach car park.

From the car park head eastwards (ie. turn right as the car park is approached on the route from the sea), following a track for about $\frac{1}{4}$ mile. The track gets rougher and ascends to Trebarvah Farm. Go through the buildings, but do not follow the lane running north: instead, turn right, over a stile and walk along the edge of a field, heading south-eastwards. Maintain direction along the right edge of a long narrow field (going over another stile), continuing to Trevean Farm. Now turn left, then right passing the farm (on your right) and head southwards along the edges of three fields to reach Acton Castle, now a hotel. On reaching the hedge, turn left and go over another stile on to a lane. Turn right along the lane, and at Trenalls House turn left to reach the starting car park.

POINTS OF INTEREST:

Prussia Cove – The Cove gets its name from the self-styled King of Prussia, one John Carter, a smuggler who operated hereabouts in the second half of the 18th century, using many of the convenient sea-caves for storage.

Cudden Point – This fine viewpoint enjoyed by travellers since the Iron Age, there being the remains of a pre-Christian fort on the Point.

St Michael's Mount – The Mount is one of the great Cornish showpieces and can be viewed in all its glory as the walk proceeds towards the village of Perranuthnoe.

REFRESHMENTS:

There are several inns, cafés and tea-rooms in Perranuthnoe.

Walk 68   GORRAN HAVEN AND THE DEADMAN   4¹/₂m (7km)

Maps: OS Sheets Landranger 204; Pathfinder 1361.
Fieldpaths and clifftop walking in South Cornwall.
Start: At 999404, the National Trust Car Park, Penare.

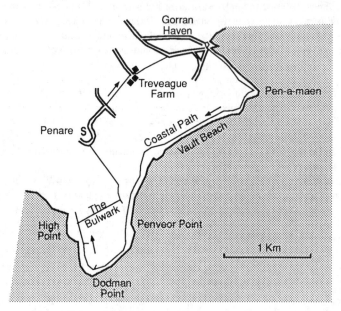

This walk commences at the small National Trust car park in Penare which is reached by turning south off the A390 St Austell-Truro road for about 9 miles. An alternative start is from the car park in Gorran Haven (though there are then no refreshment stops en route).

From Penare go back to the road junction (ie. heading north). Cross directly over and follow the signed path towards Treveague Farm, crossing two fields with the buildings of the farm ahead. Turn right along the farm lane and then go left at the signpost for Gorran Haven. Follow the track behind a house, through a gate and into a field with another reassuring signpost for Gorran Haven. Now go downhill to reach a lane and turn right to reach **Gorran Haven** itself. The alternative starting car park is passed before you start to descend to the beach.

132

After spending time admiring the harbour and beach, turn right up Foxhole Lane, following the sign indicating Vault Beach. Keep left along the easier path to reach Pen-a-maen from where there are fine views of Chapel Point, about 2 miles to the north-east, and Gribbin Head some 6 miles further off. The destination headland of **Dodman Point** is 2 miles off to the south-west, but first the route continues along Vault Beach before climbing up to a stile and seat. The section of the South West Coastal Path beyond is well-signed and easily followed: go along the bottom edge of fields and along cliff tops, then past Penveor Point and through a little wooded area. Now go over a stile and continue to the promontory of **Dodman Point** with its stone cross and old watch-house. Continue along the coast, now heading north-westwards for $^1/_4$ mile to reach a stile and gate, on the right, with a signpost indicating Penare. Follow the signed direction, going along the bank of 'The Bulwark' for a short $^1/_2$ mile, then turning northwards back to the start point in Penare.

POINTS OF INTEREST:
Gorran Haven – Once an important pilchard-fishing centre, but now a largely unspoilt holiday village with a good beach.
Dodman Point – The headland, also known as The Deadman, has the remains of an Iron Age fort, its inland ditch and bank defensive line being known as The Bulwark. A local clergyman caused the simple stone cross to be erected as a clear landmark for passing sailors in 1896. The watch-house was one of several signal stations used by the Admiralty in the 18th century.

REFRESHMENTS:
The Llawnroc Inn, Gorran Haven.
There are also several cafés in Gorran Haven.

Walk 69   HOLYWELL AND KELSEY HEAD   4$\frac{1}{2}$m (7km)

Maps: OS Sheets Landranger 200; Pathfinder 1352.

Sand dunes, clifftops and little coves.

Start: At 766590, Holywell car park.

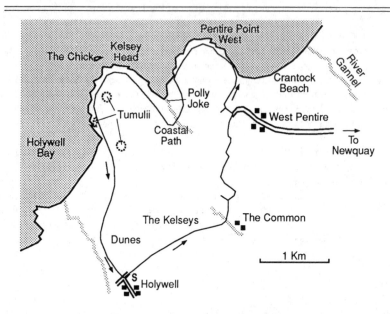

From the car park in Holywell, which lies between Perranporth and Newquay, walk a few yards northwards to the café and then turn right by the bungalows to follow a sandy track through dunes and along the edge of a golf course. Continue north-eastwards across the area known as **The Kelseys**, firstly going through a gate and then, after a mile, going through a second gate. Most of this area is National Trust property and is being planted with marram grass to keep the sand firm.

At the second gate, turn left and descend to cross a stream. Follow the clear track beyond as it zig-zags uphill alongside fields to reach a car park near the hamlet of West Pentire. Continue past the car park to reach a road junction. Turn left, westwards, and follow the signed path for West Pentire Head. Do not go off left along the Polly Joke path: instead, take the footpath on the right which leads to Pentire Point West, from where there are splendid views northwards across **Crantock Beach**.

Now continue along the South West Coastal Path (which can be steep and slippery, so take special care), going round to Polly Joke and its cove, and then continuing to Kelsey Head. The path now swings southwards and descends to the sands and **dunes** of Holywell Beach from where a boardwalk leads back to the start.

POINTS OF INTEREST:

The Kelseys – Legend has it that between Perranporth, to the south, and Newquay, to the north-east, the old city of Langarrow lies buried under the sand.

Crantock Beach – At the northern end of the beach the River Gannel empties into the sea. At one time the harbour here, now silted up, was a landing-place for travellers journeying from Brittany to Ireland who did not wish to make the hazardous route round Land's End. On Kelsey Head are a bank and ditch, all that now remains of an Iron Age fort.

Dunes – The dunes support many interesting wild flowers. The blue-green leaved sea-holly is specially interesting.

REFRESHMENTS:

There are several opportunities in Holywell.

Walk 70 MYLOR BRIDGE AND RESTRONGUET 4³/₄m (7¹/₂km)

Maps: OS Sheets Landranger 204; Pathfinder 1366.

A gentle walk round wooded tidal creeks.

Start: At 804363, Mylor Bridge car park, 3 miles north-east of
Penryn.

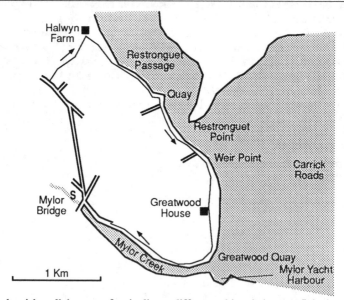

This shortish walk has very few inclines, cliffs or prehistoric interest. It is, instead, a
very pleasant stroll along river-creeks and, in due season, a splendid spring-flower
route. It also has a good pub half-way round!

Leave the car park in Mylor Bridge by walking northwards along Bells Hill for
³/₄ mile to reach a junction with the road leading right to Restronguet. Bear left, and
after a further ¹/₄ mile, turn right along a track heading north-eastwards across fields
to Halwyn Farm. On reaching a junction of lanes just short of the farm buildings, turn
right and continue along the creek-side for ³/₄ mile to reach the quay and little beach
at **Restronguet Passage**.

Maintain the same south-eastwards course alongside the River Carnon, passing
Restronguet Point on the far shore. After a further ¹/₂ mile you will arrive at Weir Point,

136

with the deep harbour of **Carrick Roads** off to the left. The walk now swings a little right, passes the gates of Greatwood House and continues southwards to reach Greatwood Quay, with Mylor Yacht Harbour, once a Naval dockyard, across the creek.

The walk concludes by following Mylor Creek, heading north-westwards for a full mile. Go past an old quarry to reach a gate. Go through and keep left of houses beyond, on the outskirts of Mylor Bridge. Soon you join Travellan Road: follow it to return to the start.

POINTS OF INTEREST:
Restronguet Passage – The name derives from a row-boat ferry that once crossed from here to Feock.
Carrick Roads – This superb anchorage, the world's third largest natural harbour, is formed by the estuaries of the Carnon, Fal and Tresillian rivers.

REFRESHMENTS:
The Pandora Inn, Restronguet Passage.
There are also possibilities at Mylor Bridge.

Walk 71   LOOE POOL – THE PENROSE WALKS   5m (8km)
Maps: OS Sheets Landranger 203; Pathfinder 1369.
An easy walk with plenty of bird-watching opportunities.
Start: At 639259, the National Trust car park, Penrose.

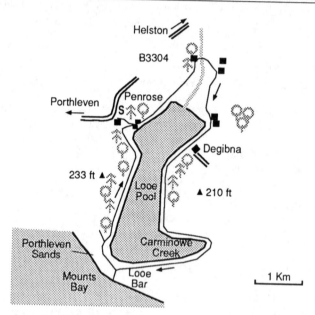

Leave the car park at Penrose, on the B3304 west of Porthleven through the gate into the estate and follow the drive, keeping **The Looe Pool** to your right. The walk is first south-eastwards, then north-eastwards through mixed woodland. After a little more than a mile, turn right through a gate on to a causeway, using it to cross the marsh and the River Cober before swinging south along a farm track.

After about ½ mile the farm at Degibna is reached. From here, the route continues southwards, alongside the Pool again. Go over a stile and follow the shore, through pines at first, then, beyond another stile, through pasture. The path keeps to the shoreline, heading east and then west to go around Carminowe Creek and then continue down to the beach at **Looe Bar**. To return to the car park, go up the ramp, through the gates, and head northwards into the estate, going through woods for about $1^1/_2$ miles to rejoin the outward drive near the car park.

POINTS OF INTEREST:
The Looe Pool – Also called The Loe, this is the largest natural lake in Cornwall cut off from often wild waters of Mounts Bay by a sand and shingle bar similar to those at Chesil Beach and Slapton Sands. Along the reedy shore herons, ducks, terns and warblers abound. The estate is especially beautiful in spring and summer when palms, rhododendrons and wild flowers surround old cottages and enhance the paths around the pool.
Looe Bar – The bar forms part of Porthleven Sands, a place to linger on a warm day. As a result, this short walk may take some time!

REFRESHMENTS:
There are none on the route but a variety of inns and restaurants can be found in nearby Helston and Porthleven.

Walk 72   PORTHPEAN AND BLACK HEAD   5m (8km)

Maps: OS Sheets Landranger 204; Pathfinder 1361.

A short, but fairly strenuous, walk with paddling opportunities.

Start: At 032507, the car park in Lower Porthpean.

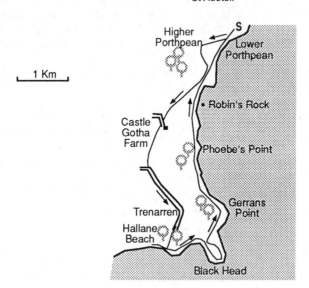

St Austell

Higher
Porthpean

Lower
Porthpean

S

1 Km

• Robin's Rock

Castle
Gotha
Farm

Phoebe's Point

Gerrans
Point

Trenarren

Hallane
Beach

Black Head

Although only 5 miles long, this walk is likely to take quite a time to negotiate its steepish cliffs and tempting beaches. The start is at Lower Porthpean, about two miles south of St Austell.

From the car park, turn right along a steep and narrow road to reach Higher Porthpean. Pass the village pump and, at Court Cottage, turn left along a path, going through the first of many kissing gates (so take a suitable companion!). Walk parallel to the cliff path, and at the next kissing gate, in the hedge to the right, go through and cross the field beyond to pass the farmhouse of Castle Gotha Farm, on your left. Maintain direction (southwards), following waymarks across a farm lane (more kissing gates!) and more fields. Eventually you will reach the seventh gate. Just beyond, keep the hedge to the left to reach kissing gate Number Eight: go through on to a

140

usually quiet road offering splendid views, to the left, across St Austell Bay to Gribbin Head. Bear right along the road, following it through the hamlets of Trenarren and Hallane, and at the entrance to Hallane House descend a woodland track to the beach.

After a deserved rest (sandwiches? thermos?), return uphill to the signed Coastal Path. Turn right and follow it steeply up to the view point at **Black Head**. Retrace the track to turn northwards around The Bite, Gerrans Point and Ropehaven Nature Reserve to reach the car park at Trenarren. Go over the stile and descend steeply to a bridge. Cross and go up the steps on the far side to Silvermine Point – another resting place with grand views. Continue to follow the Coastal Path, northwards, passing Phoebe's Point and Robin's Rock and then descending to the beach, which invites warm feet and refreshments, and the start.

POINTS OF INTEREST:

Black Head – A superb viewpoint – south across Mevagissey Bay to Chapel Point, eastwards to Gribbin Head and further off to Rame Head. There was a settlement here in Iron Age times so the views have been appreciated for over 3,000 years.

Along the cliffs, indeed on all the sections of the South West Peninsula Coastal Walk, wild flowers grow plentifully. Appreciate them, check them in your wildflower book but don't pick! And please remember after you have enjoyed your packed lunch to leave no litter.

REFRESHMENTS:

Nothing on the route so take your own and enjoy it at one of the viewpoints or beaches. There is a beach café at Porthpean and there are plenty of restaurants and inns in St Austell.

Walk 73   CAPE CORNWALL AND THE COT VALLEY   5m (8km)

Maps: OS Sheets Landranger 203; Explorer 7.

Industrial ghosts, a pretty valley and a stretch of cliff-path.

Start: At 371314, St Just-in-Penwith Church.

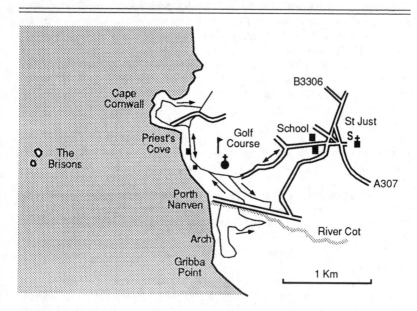

St Just lies on the A307 about 8 miles north of Land's End. From the church, take the road for Cape Cornwall, heading westwards to pass the school. At a junction, fork left along Carn Gloose Road aiming for a lonely chimney about $^1/_2$ mile further on. About 100 yards before the chimney, turn sharp left and descend. Go over stiles and then steeply down a walled path. After making right and left turns you will reach a road: turn right and walk down to Porth Nanven, with its adjacent coves and rocky beach.

Cross the little bridge on the left and strike southwards, climbing to the clifftop and observing several old mine ruins off to the left. Please do not be tempted to explore - the area is dangerous. It is better to enjoy the splendid seascapes to the right, where The Brisons stand about $^3/_4$ mile off shore. These rocks have been responsible for many shipwrecks over the centuries.

Just before reaching Gribba Point, about $1/2$ mile from Porth Nanven, turn left, inland, along a clear path. The path turns left and right before reaching the little River Cot. Follow the river westwards again almost back to Porth Nanven, but before then, cross to pass between two sharp boulders. Now climb up a stony track towards the cliffs, heading northwards this time. Again there are many signs of mining just inland to the right, but you should not climb the fence to explore. Instead, aim for the cliff path and follow it to the coastguard cottages and lighthouse at Cape Cornwall, passing above Priest's Cove.

Follow the path as it circuits around the Cape, with the Bristol Channel ahead and Land's End back left, to reach a road. Turn right to complete the circuit, heading back southwards towards the chimney stack once more. Go past the Ballowall Barrow and then turn left to retrace the outward route back along Carn Gloose Road into St Just.

POINTS OF INTEREST:

St Just – The village was once an important mining centre where tin, copper and arsenic was extracted from hundreds of deep shafts (some over 2,000 feet – 610m), with adits stretching under the sea. It is said that during stormy weather the miners could hear rocks on the sea-bed above them shifting in the heavy seas. As well as the sturdy granite church there is a large Methodist Chapel – a reminder of Wesley's strong influence here in the South West.

The cairns and barrows which abound along the cliffs are evidence of a Bronze Age population.

To savour further the past days of mining the walker might like to visit the Geevor Heritage Centre, near Pendeen on B3306 a few miles north of St Just, where there are opportunities to go underground. The mine is very popular in summer and you may have to book (tel: 01736-788662).

The Botallack engine houses, about $3/4$ mile north of St Just, have also been restored recently.

REFRESHMENTS:

There are several excellent possibilities in St Just.

Walk 74   GUNNISLAKE AND CHILSWORTHY   5m (8km)

Maps: OS Sheets Landranger 201; Pathfinder 1340.

Quiet lanes, riverbanks and evidence of old mine workings.

Start: At 434722, New Bridge, Gunnislake.

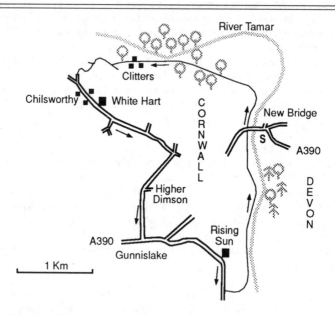

This walk begins in Devon - just - but is almost all in Cornwall. The bridge across the Tamar dates from 1520 and needs to be the height it is as the river rises in times of flood by many feet. The river bank paths are very muddy and often flooded so this walk is only possible after dry spells.

Cross the bridge, heading westward into Cornwall, and turn right just before the garage to walk along the river bank. The path turns away from the river fairly soon and heads westwards through woodland to reach an area that was once very busy, as evidenced by the many old shafts and tips, though these are now overgrown. It is not wise to stray too far from the path.

The river's meanders have now returned it to the path: continue until you are about a mile from the walk's start, where there is a gate. Go through, turn right and drop down to a T-junction. Turn left and ascend to reach a lane. Turn left and follow the lane to the outskirts of Chilsworthy, an old mining village. Walk past the White Hart Inn, continuing to reach a junction. Keep straight on, and at the next junction keep straight on again to reach a crossroads. Turn right and walk downhill, passing Higher Dimson before reaching the main road, the A390, at Gunnislake. Turn left, with care, towards the railway station.

Go under the railway bridge and turn right into Well Park Road. Go along the road for about 100 yards to reach a white gate. There, turn left and descend. After a further $1/_4$ mile, at a T-junction, turn left to reach the Rising Sun Inn, on the right. Continue downhill for another $1/_4$ mile to reach the River Tamar. Fork left and then go left again to follow the riverbank for almost 2 miles back to New Bridge.

POINTS OF INTEREST:

There was once a plan to link this area by canal to the Bude canal system thus forming a waterway from the Bristol Channel to Plymouth, but this was abandoned. The Clitters Mine and the Great Consols Mine, both on the Devon bank of the river, were but two of the most productive copper, tin and arsenic sources in all Europe.

REFRESHMENTS:

The White Hart Inn, Chilsworthy.
The Rising Sun Inn, Gunnislake.

Walk 75   BROWN WILLY AND ROUGH TOR   5½m (9km)

Maps: OS Sheets Landranger 200 and 201; Pathfinder 1338.

A demanding walk to Cornwall's highest point on Bodmin Moor.
Start: At 138819, the car park at the end of the lane, south-east of Camelford.

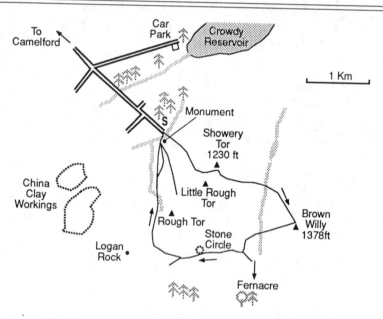

This is another walk requiring stout boots, a knowledge of how to use a map and compass, some determination and a fine weather forecast! The result should bring splendid views, a sense of achievement and the nearest approach to hill walking in Cornwall. To avoid the moor's peat bogs, remember that the really unpleasant bits are dark brown.

From the car park, walk across the bridge over the stream and head south-eastwards, uphill, aiming for the left end of the ridge ahead. After about ¼ mile, bear a little left (eastwards) to reach three great boulders one on top of another – Showery Tor at 1,230 feet (375m). Little Rough Tor is the summit off to the right – the route, however, is south-eastwards again. After about ¼ mile, cross a stream (the ground here is often boggy) and then ascend, bearing right for a further $^1/_4$ mile to reach the trig. point on top of **Brown Willy** (1,378 feet – 420m). On a good day the view from here extends northwards to the Bristol Channel and southwards to the English Channel, with wild and lonely Bodmin Moor stretching on all sides.

From the summit, turn a little south of due west to cross the stream again. Now follow a wall around to reach a clear track coming from the south (Fernacre). Now go right, heading for an ancient stone circle. On reaching the circle, maintain direction for about 250 yards before leaving the track, turning right by a ruined cottage and heading north to the **Logan Rock**, perched on other rocks at the summit of Louden Hill. Off to the left are odd-looking china-clay workings, while to the right are the weirdly-eroded rock formations of Rough Tor, and evidence of ancient settlements and cairns.

Now head due north, making for the right-hand end of a wall. Cross a stream but stay on the track to the right of the water, passing a **Monument** on the return to the start. It may well be that the final few hundred yards are very soggy: if so keep to the right where another path, coming from Rough Tor, can be joined for the final stretch.

POINTS OF INTEREST:

Brown Willy – The curious name derives from the Celtic *bron ewhella* – highest hill.
Logan Rock – Logans are balanced rocks created by erosion which rock when pushed slightly. The rocking is said to foretell the future to those who can 'read' the motion.
Monument – This is a memorial to Charlotte Dymond. She had a crippled lover who was hung for her brutal and bloody murder on the moor hereabouts – some say he was innocent however. 'Tis said she haunts the area so make sure the walk is completed before dark!

REFRESHMENTS:

Nothing en route, but nearby Camelford has inns, a restaurant and a café.

Walk 76   CAMELFORD AND WATERGATE   5½m (9km)

Maps: OS Sheets Landranger 200; Pathfinder 1325.

An agricultural walk – farms, farm implements and fine views.

Start: At 104836, the car park at the Information Centre, Camelford.

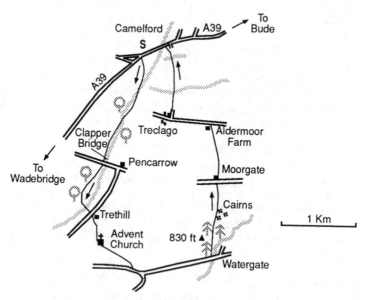

From the Information Centre in **Camelford**, walk south along the main road and under the arch inscribed *River and Advent Church*. Now go along the bank of the River Camel for a mile, using footbridges where necessary, to reach the **Clapper Bridge**.

Here, turn right but take the gate, left, and follow the signed footpath across fields. Go over a stone stile and descend into woodland. Emerging from the wood after ¼ mile, cross a footbridge over the Camel and walk up to the gate ahead, by Trethin Manor. Go through on to a road and turn right. After just a few yards, cross a stile on the left and head towards the church (**Advent Church**) at Tresinney.

After exploring, leave the churchyard through a little gate on the eastern side and follow the footpath beyond, heading south-eastwards over stiles to reach a lane. Turn left and follow the lane to Watergate. The bridge here is a spot to linger for a while. To continue with the walk, go back along the lane for a few yards and take the signed footpath on the right, heading northwards through meadows to reach a small pine plantation. Go over a stile, and follow waymarkers past cairns, to the right, and around the barn and buildings of Moorgate Farm to reach a road. Cross the road and follow the signed path opposite, reached by going over steps in the wall. Follow the path, still heading northwards for $^1/_4$ mile, descending to reach a lane at Aldermoor Farm.

Turn left (westwards) along the lane towards Treclago, but just before the scattered settlement is reached, turn right along another lane. This lane soon becomes a track: follow it into a field. Go through a gate and head straight towards Camelford about $^1/_3$ mile ahead. Go over a footbridge and a stile to reach a lane which is followed to the A39. Turn left back to the Museum and Information Centre at the start.

POINTS OF INTEREST:

Camelford – Despite the town hall's weather-vane it is sheep, not camel, country hereabouts!

During your visit to the town, do not miss the North Cornwall Museum, housed in an old coach house – a well-deserved prize-winner for the best small museum in Britain. The locals claim Camelford is the Camelot of King Arthur – but there are many other similar claimants in the West Country.

Clapper Bridge – Made of great slabs of local stone (usually granite) such bridges abound in Devon and Cornwall. They are probably very old indeed.

Advent Church – Note the tower with its eight pinnacles. The church is mostly a 15th-century construction, but inside there is a 12th-century font.

REFRESHMENTS:

There are numerous possibilities in Camelford.

Maps: OS Sheets Landranger 201; Pathfinder 1356.
Cliff walks, farm and woodland paths – a figure of eight walk that can be completed as two single walks.
Start: At 432503, Kingsand car park.

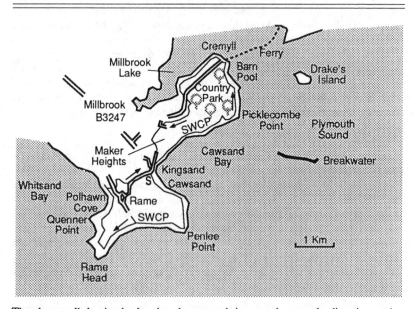

The short walk begins by leaving the car park in a south-westerly direction, going through **Cawsand** and passing its church, to the left. Go up the lane and through trees to emerge on to the Coastal Path. Now follow the Path, heading south-eastwards at first and enjoying sea views across Cawsand Bay and the Plymouth Breakwater. Ignore all the paths off to the right (inland) maintaining direction along the cliffs, occasionally going over stiles and through gorse. In due course the path rounds Penlee Point and heads westwards: after a long mile a short diversion (¹/₄ mile) inland leads to the medieval church at Rame. The route continues along the cliff path to reach a left fork, with steps, up to the fascinating little Chapel of St Michael and **Rame Head** itself. The route continues along the Coastal Path, with fine views ahead across Whitsand Bay and, after passing Queener Point, down into Polhawn Cove. As the Coastal Path swings a little inland, by some buildings, turn right into Rame. Now to return to Kingsand, follow the lane downhill for a short $1/_2$ mile, and at the junction keep right for a further $1/_2$ mile back to the car park.

The longer walk continues by going downhill to the inn and beach at Kingsand and then left along the rocky shore, heading north-eastwards. After a $1/_4$ mile, by some old ruined buildings, turn left through bushes into a field. Bear right to gain the top corner and go through a gap on to a track. Now keep right and you will soon pick up the Coastal Path with its acorn signs. Head eastwards and then northwards, and ultimately go through rhododendron bushes – a total distance of 2 miles – to reach Picklecombe Point. After passing a stone arch, fork right and descend almost to the water's edge below 'Lady Emma's Cottage'. Now head northwards, with the deer park and grounds of the Country Park to the left. The Park invites wandering diversions and there is a House to visit, but the walk continues down to the ferry landing at Cremyll. On arriving at the car park, walk down the road and turn left at the telephone box, by the Edgcumbe Arms. Now follow the direction-post signed 'Empacombe', keeping left at an old chapel and turning right at the next junction. At a second post (with instructions to follow), go through the gate, round a mini-harbour, across the grass and through a second gate. Now cross the B3247, with care, and go directly forward into a field, through a gate, obeying the sign 'To Maker'. The farm track beyond runs parallel to the road for a short distance, then goes uphill and to the right, towards a wooded area. Now follow the waymarks to Maker Church. From the western end of the church, make for the stile in the wall and cross several fields (separated by walls and stiles). Go through a gate to emerge on to a lane. Go directly across and over yet another stile. Now cross two fields to join a lane, following it as it descends, with encouraging signposts, to reach **Kingsand** and the beach. From here it is a short step back to the start.

POINTS OF INTEREST:
Cawsand and Kingsand – These villages, with their numerous inns, were very popular with men of the fleet – at Plymouth – as ships anchored off shore before the breakwater was built.
Rame Head – Before the Eddystone Light (9 miles SSW) was built, a fire beacon was maintained at Rame Head by a monk who lived in the chapel.

REFRESHMENTS:
The Edgcumbe Arms, Cremyll
There is also a wide selection in Cawsand and Kingsand.

Walk 79 LAND'S END 6m (9¹/₂km)

Maps: OS Sheets Landranger 203; Pathfinder 1368.

Steep bits and dramatic cliff tops at England's furthest westerly point.

Start: At 355263, the car park in Sennen Cove.

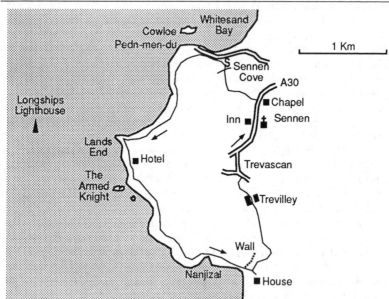

From the car park at **Sennen Cove**, walk westwards with Whitesand Bay to the right. Go past the lifeboat station and the public toilets and ascend, keeping right when the footpath forks. Now follow the Coastal Path, looking right towards America, and ahead and right to the first and last pub at **Land's End**, with, nearby, the very comprehensive signpost. Continue southwards, then south-eastwards, climbing and descending to reach Mill Bay (also known as Nanjizal) where there are granite-bouldered enclosures. About 200 yards before a single house with ground floor bay windows, the path crosses a broken wall. About 40-50 yards past this, fork left and then, 70 yards further on, go sharp left, ascending on a not-very-distinct path. This path soon descends into a little valley, passes a granite wall, to the left, and crosses a footbridge.

Keep right at the next fork, maintaining the north-easterly course through gorse for about 220 yards. Then, on reaching another wall, to the left, keep with it until a set of stone steps is reached. Use these to climb the wall into a large field. Turn half-left, leaving the wall and making for the hill-top ahead. Now go straight on to reach the left-hand field corner. Turn right along the right edge of the next field and maintain this northerly direction, going through a gateway and then through the farm buildings of Trevilley to emerge on to a lane at a T-junction.

Go straight over, climb stone steps, go through another farmyard and negotiate more stone steps. Now go along the right edge of a field (with telephone poles on the other side of the wall) and go over a stone stile at the end. Walk along the left edge of the next field heading directly towards the houses in the hamlet of Trevascan. Take the gate through a garden to reach a road. Turn left for 300 yards, then go right at a junction. Follow the road for 200 yards to reach the main A30. Turn right, with great care, and proceed along the A30 for $^1/_4$ mile to reach the inn, to the left, and the church, to the right, at **Sennen**. Go past the cemetery and, opposite the chapel, take the footpath on the left, heading north-westwards towards the buildings on the outskirts of Sennen Cove. On reaching a lane, turn right to reach the starting car park.

POINTS OF INTEREST:

Sennen Cove – This was once a fishing village, but little now remains from that time. Whitesand Bay is a popular holiday resort and the RNLI station is worth a visit.
Land's End – Westward is the Longships Lighthouse – about $1^1/_2$ miles offshore and visible on a clear day. The Scilly Isles (27 miles away) are sometimes visible too. America is further and invisible. The Land's End Complex provides interesting information, but above all, the spectacle of the surging Atlantic meeting the mainland.
Sennen – The church of St Sennen boasts of being the most westerly in England. Its fine tower of granite is an excellent marker for ships at sea. Nearby is an ancient wayside cross.

REFRESHMENTS:

The First and Last Inn, Land's End.
There are also possibilities in Sennen.

Walks 80 & 81   **LIZARD POINT**   6m (9¹/₂km)
or 10m (16km)

Maps: OS Sheets Landranger 203; Pathfinder 1372.
Superb cliff and country walking around the 'furthest south' of mainland Britain.
Start: At 703125, Lizard village, at the end of the A3083.

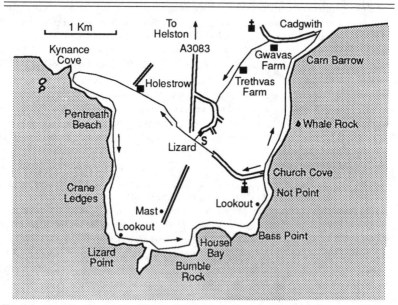

The whole walk takes in the village of **Lizard**, the popular beach at Kynance Cove, a section of the South West Coastal Path and the fisherman's hamlet of Cadgwith. The shorter walk turns inland about 2 miles short of Cadgwith, approximately halving the whole distance. It would, of course, be possible to walk from Lizard due east to Church Cove and then follow the coastal path to Cadgwith thus making a third alternative walk of about 4¹/₂ miles.

From Lizard walk westwards along the lane signposted for **Kynance Cove**. On reaching a set of stone steps by a chalet, half-right, take them, continuing to reach a road junction. Follow the 'Kynance Cove' signposts again, passing Holestrow and descending to the Cove. After suitable rest and enjoyment, turn east to following the

Coastal Path past the Crane Ledger to reach Lizard Point. Continue due east to reach the lighthouse. Beyond, the Coastal Path around Housel Bay to reach Bass Point, this section offering particularly splendid seascapes. Continue past the old Lloyds signal station and the lifeboat house to reach Church Cove.

The shorter walk turns left here, going past the first house after the lifeboat station and ascending a lane. Go past **St Wynalow's Church** and continue back to Lizard.

The longer walk continues northwards along the Coastal Path to reach **Cadgwith**. This is a long $1^1/_2$ miles, though the Devil's Frying Pan offers a useful stopping point before the descent into Cadgwith with its picture-postcard cottages and refreshment opportunities. From the village, retrace the route for a few hundred yards to a house called 'Hillside'. There, turn right up Prazegooth Lane to reach a set of garages. Here bear right to reach a road. Turn left (signed 'Lizard $3^1/_2$') and follow the road to Gwavas Farm. Now, as the road turns right, go straight ahead, follow signs to reach a stile. Go up the stone steps in a wall and along an access lane beyond to reach Trethvas Farm. The village of Lizard is seen clearly ahead now: go along field-edges and over stiles to reach a road. Turn left. Ignore left turnings to Church Cove, continuing ahead to reach Beacon Terrace and the village square where the walk started.

POINTS OF INTEREST:
Lizard – A village full of 'tourist attractions' which can be very busy in the summer. Lizard Point, $^3/_4$ mile south of the village centre, is the nearest point to the equator on mainland Britain. The lighthouse is open to the public. The whole area enjoys a very mild climate so the botanist, as well as the geologist, will find much to enjoy.
Kynance Cove – The Cove is justly famous for its photogenic charm and serpentine rocks and islets.
St Wynalow's Church – The church has a special claim to fame in that, in 1670, the last sermon in the Cornish Language was preached here.
Cadgwith – Fishermen's cottages, a small chapel and a good inn make this village an attractive target for the walker. The Devil's Frying Pan nearby was created by the collapse of a sea cave.

REFRESHMENTS:
There are numerous possibilities in Lizard and Cadgwith, and a hotel at Housel Bay.

Walks 82 & 83   MULLION AND KYNANCE COVES   6m (9½km)
or 9½m (15km)

Maps: OS Sheets Landranger 203; Explorer 8.
Splendid Cornish coastal scenery - a naturalists' 'special'.
Start: At 688133, the car park at Kynance Cove.

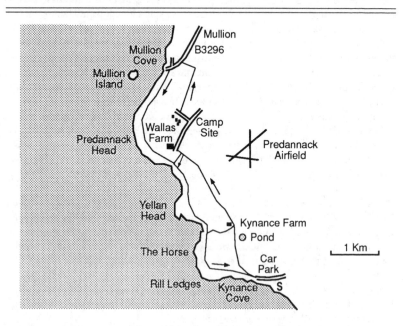

From the very popular car park near **Kynance Cove,** fork right – away from the South
West Coastal Path which goes north-westwards along the cliff path - making instead
for the clear footpath running north across the downland to Kynance Farm about ½
mile distant. The walled track is ancient and bordered by wild flowers. Pass to the left
of a pond and to the right of the farm buildings. Now do not take the path going left,
temptingly, towards the cliffs: instead maintain the north-north-westward direction
along the track, passing a barn, to the left. As the track turns right towards Predannack
Airfield, turn left and walk parallel to the coast for a long mile towards the buildings
of Wollas Farm.

156

Just before the farm the shorter walk turns left. Walk for about 350 yards, with a little stream to your right, to reach the South West Coastal Path above Ogo-dour Cove. Here the longer walk is rejoined.

The longer walk continues to Wollas Farm. There, take the lane leading back towards the airfield, reaching a junction after about $1/_4$ mile. Turn left, but after 300 yards, by another farm, on the left, turn right and descend towards a tumulus. Now go towards the stream and buildings at **Mullion Cove**. Turn left, downhill, along the lane and follow it to the seashore. There now follows almost 5 miles of wonderful cliff walking, following the Coastal Path over Predannack Cliffs and Vallan Head to rejoin the shorter walk at Ogo-dour. There is the occasional stream and stile and one or two steep ups and downs, but the views are stunning and the area abounds with kittiwakes, gulls, ravens, razorbills and many other seabirds. Wild flowers include Cornish heath, gorse, broom and clover, and these are home to many butterflies, including the monarch and other rarities.

After the shorter walk has been rejoined, the route continues along the Coastal Path, following it past **Rill**, and then down to Kynance Cove and the start.

POINTS OF INTEREST:

Kynance Cove – The Cove is justly famous for its sea-sculpted features, sands and multi-coloured serpentine rocks which are carved into semi-precious jewellery locally.
Mullion Cove – With its solid granite harbour walls, old net store building and wooden fish cellar, the Cove has all necessary features to enchant the photographer and sketcher. Thyme and sea-thrift are common hereabouts.
Rill – It was from this headland that the Spanish Armada was first sighted in 1588.

Apart from seabirds mentioned above, the keen watcher will probably see lapwing, larks, pipits, stonechats, wheatears, buzzards, and possibly even harriers and sparrowhawks.

REFRESHMENTS:

There are sometimes ice-cream vans at Kynance and there are an inn and tea-rooms in Mullion, but if it is a warm day you will need to take something along with you!

Walk 84   THE ROSELAND PENINSULA   6m (9½km)

Maps: OS Sheets Landranger 204; Explorer 8.

A fairly easy walk around the peninsula south-east of Falmouth.
Start: At 848312, the St Anthony Head car park.

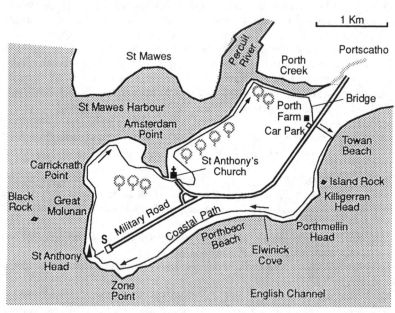

From the National Trust car park (a fee is payable by non-members) walk southwards to the **Lighthouse at St Anthony Head**. Now go right, northwards, with Black Rock off to the left and the headland of Carricknath Point ahead. Keep on the well-signed Coastal Path, at first passing through National Trust land and then using a boardwalk across an old dam. Descend to the beach at Great Molunan, then climb up again, continuing north-eastwards, with St Mawes across the bay to the left. On approaching a wooded area, before reaching Amsterdam Point, turn right (still following the Coastal Path) and ascend to reach a stile.

Go over and descend along the left edge of a field. At the bottom, go left over another stile and then right along a clear track to reach the entrance to Place House. There, fork right and ascend to the **churchyard**. Go through the churchyard, leave over the stile at the eastern end. Now follow the sign for 'Coastal Path Place Quay'. From the quay, go over another stile and follow the sign for 'Porth Farm $1^1/_2$ m '. Go through a plantation and maintain the northerly direction along the creek-side, avoiding the temptation to go right, inland. Go into woodland, then walk alongside Porth Creek. Again resist the temptation to take the inland path (the right-hand path towards Bohortha), continuing to reach a stile at the end of the woods. Cross and go forward to reach a footbridge. Cross this and then go right for $^3/_4$ mile to reach Porth Farm and its car park.

Cross the road and head south-eastwards, following the sign 'To the Beach', following the path down to Towan. This sandy spot is a good place to linger before the final part of the walk. This final section begins by heading southwards: go through a kissing-gate and follow the Coastal Path past Killigerran Head and Porthmellin. The Path now turns westward above Elwinick Cove and Porthbeor Beach: continue along it for a further 2 miles of splendid clifftop walking to reach Zone Point. It is now just a short step to the start, which is just inland from the lighthouse.

POINTS OF INTEREST:
The Lighthouse at St Anthony Head – The lighthouse often sounds loud warning blasts which could surprise the innocent walker - beware!
Churchyard – St Anthony's Church is part Norman and part medieval.

The creeks on this walk are good places for the bird-watcher - look out for redshank, oyster-catchers and curlews.
The whole of the walk also offers good opportunities for photographs, so be sure to take your camera.

REFRESHMENTS:
May be available at the car parks and Towan Beach 'in the season'. Otherwise you will need to take your own or visit St Mawes or Portscatho after completing the walk.

Walk 85   CRACKINGTON HAVEN $6^1/_2$m (10km)

Maps: OS Sheets Landranger 190; Pathfinder 1310.

A wooded streamside valley, some farm paths and Cornwall's highest cliffs.

Start: At 143968, Crackington Haven.

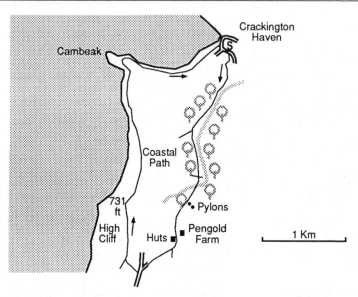

Take the road out of **Crackington Haven** – which lies 7 miles north of Boscastle – heading southwards towards Boscastle. Ignore the road on the right signed 'High Cliff', but take the next right, a farm track. On arriving at the farm, go straight on to reach a waymarked gate (**NOT** downhill right and uphill left!) and go through into woodland. After a short $^1/_4$ mile, cross a bridge and keep right, as signed for 'Woodgates' (**NOT** as signed for 'Hallagather'). Go over a second bridge and turn left, south-westwards, to follow yellow waymarkers through the woods to reach another signpost (indicating 'Woodgate', to the right). Here, go half-left, southwards again, on a path soon signed 'Sheepdip'. The woodland path emerges into more open land, but soon returns into the trees: keep straight on at a cross-junction, following the sign

160

for 'Pengold', go over a stream and turn right, uphill, towards two electricity pylons. On reaching these, bear a little right, ascending to reach a gate. Take the track to the left across a field to reach Pengold Farm.

Now, obeying the signs, go through the farm buildings, with Nissen huts to the right, and turn right along the access lane, heading south-westwards to reach the coast road. Turn left along the road, but after 100 yards go right, climbing the steps by the National Trust sign to reach the **Coastal Path** at **High Cliff**. Adventurous walkers might like to try the views from the very edge of the cliff, but the safer path is a little inland (although still with superb views). Follow the Path for an exhilarating $2\frac{1}{2}$ miles, heading northwards and then eastwards, back to Crackington Haven.

POINTS OF INTEREST:
Crackington Haven – The Haven comprises a pleasant beach of dark sand, two car parks and a churchyard 'extra' of unconsecrated ground for the bodies of shipwrecked sailors of unknown religious faiths.

Coastal Path – This walk takes in a short section of the central part of the 500 mile South-West Peninsula Coastal Path which begins at Minehead, in Somerset and ends in Poole, in Dorset. The Path largely follows coastguard footpaths and is seldom far from habitation a few miles inland. It is often subject to strong winds or mists and walkers need to take appropriate precautions in such conditions.

High Cliff – The 730 foot cliffs are the highest in Cornwall and offer views north to the nearby Cambeak and Hartland Point, further off. To the south the headlands of Boscastle and Tintagel are distinct on clear days.

REFRESHMENTS:
The Compass Inn, Crackington Haven,

Walk 86   **BODINNICK AND POLRUAN**   6½m (10km)

Maps: OS Sheets Landranger 200; Pathfinder 1354.

A scenic walk, with cliff tops, beaches, estuaries, woodland and two fine villages.

Start: At 130521, Bodinnick ferry landing.

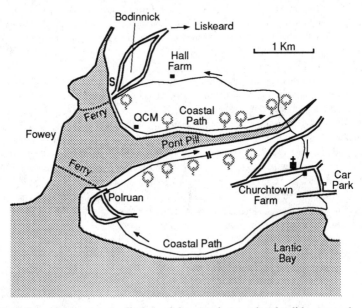

This walk, with many steep climbs and descents but much splendid scenery, begins at Bodinnick where the ferry lands from **Fowey**.

Turn south along the South West Coastal Path, which here is a tree-lined walk offering an interesting contrast between shipping and the activity connected with the china-clay industry on the far shore westward. Follow the path as it turns left, eastwards, about ½ mile from the ferry, passing the Quiller-Couch Memorial and continuing for about a mile to reach a stile. Go over, turn right and descend, heading south again, to cross the bridge over the Pont Pill. Now ascend, maintaining the southerly direction, along a woodland path, reaching a road at the top of the rise. Turn left, downhill, then turn right, into a field, through the right-hand of two gates.

The path beyond heads uphill to reach a lane by a lonely church. Bear right to follow the lane past Churchtown Farm, still ascending, then bear right again to reach a car park. Continue along the lane to a junction. Turn right along the lane for 100 yards, then go left over a stile. Cross the field beyond and then continue seawards to reach the Coastal Path again.

Turn right and follow the Coastal Path westwards, above Lantic Bay, for $1^1/_2$ miles to reach a road. Turn right and follow the road, soon bearing left to reach a more major road. Go left and downhill into **Polruan**. After enjoying a rest and refreshments at the interesting spot near the ferry terminal, ascend the main road again for about 350 yards. Now look out for a set of steps leading up beside No. 73. Take these: the path beyond goes downhill, bearing left to reach the Pont Pill estuary again, but now on the opposite shore to that reached on the earlier stage of the walk. Continue along the shore, but after about $^1/_3$ mile, turn right and cross a drive. Now head north-eastwards, through woodland, ignoring all paths off to the right, to reach a road. Now keep ahead along the National Trust path, with a hedge on your right, to reach Pont Pill bridge again.

Cross the bridge, then bear right, uphill, before bearing left through woodland to reach a stile. Cross and ascend the field beyond, bearing a little left to reach a gate. Go through and continue westwards, with a hedge on the right, to reach two gates. Go through the right-hand one and head downhill to Hall Farm. Keeping the barn on your right, walk due west through the farm and then descend to the War Memorial in Bodinnick. Here, a right turn leads back to the ferry.

POINTS OF INTEREST:

Fowey – The port here handles shipments of Cornwall's principal industry – china-clay. Wheal Martyn Museum at Carthew, 2 miles north of St Austell, has a very full explanation of the industry and exhibits on local history: a most interesting day can be spent there.

Polruan – A 'typical Cornish village' in which to linger. Lantic Bay, with its cliffs and beaches, is an attractive area to picnic or laze on the beach, and is also excellent for wild-flower spotting.

REFRESHMENTS:

There are inns and cafés in Fowey, Polruan and Bodinnick.

Walk 87   COVERACK AND ST KEVERNE   6¹/₂m (10km)

Maps: OS Sheets Landranger 204; Pathfinder 1370.

Cornish countryside and a stretch of coastal path. Easy, but many stiles.

Start: At 783187, the car park in Coverack.

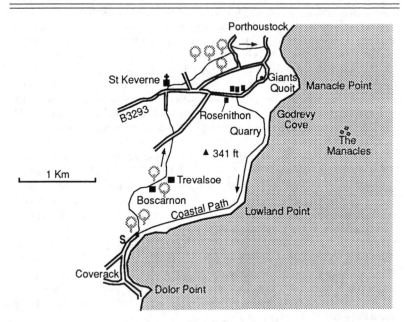

From the car park, take the lane leading north out of **Coverack**, with the English Channel off to the right. As the built-up area ends, follow a path which forks left and inland, ascending to reach a grassy area. Now take the narrow track between stone walls, following it through woodland. The trees give way to hedges as the route turns right into a field: continue with a hedge on the left. Maintain direction to reach a stile. Cross on to the lane leading to Boscarnon Farm and, further on, Trevalsoe Farm.

Cross a stile on the left, and continue northwards, with a hedge on the right, to reach a second stile. Cross and again walk with a hedge to the right. Now, as the hedge turns off to the right, walk half-right across the field to reach a third stile. Go over and keep a hedge to the right yet again to reach another stile. Cross and now

164

walk with a hedge to the left to reach a fifth stile. Cross and maintain direction across the field beyond to emerge on to the road. Here a short detour to the right will bring you to a welcome farm selling ice-cream and fudge.

The walk continues by going straight over the road and crossing yet another stile. Go half-right across the field beyond, with a hedge to the right, then walk beside two more fields to reach an access road which is followed to the pretty village of St Keverne with its square and church.

Go through the churchyard, left, then right and, on exiting, follow a path which descends eastwards to reach a lane. Go straight over and maintain the easterly direction as you descend into a wooded valley. On reaching the next road, turn left, uphill, for a short distance, then go right to continue descending towards the beach at Porthoustock.

Soon, bear right up a steep road, heading southwards, and then take the first left. Now follow the Coastal Path sign, crossing a stile, on the right, and going half-left across a field, passing the curious Giant's Quoit, to the left, and continuing to reach a road. Turn right along the road, following it to a group of buildings, Rosenithon. Turn left along a little lane. This soon becomes a track: bear left into a field and then emerge, right, on to the splendid cliff path. Now follow the Coastal Path, with the **Manacles Rocks** out to sea, to return to Coverack.

POINTS OF INTEREST:

Coverack – Much of the rock hereabouts is serpentine, a colourful, hard rock made into souvenirs. Goonhilly, the Satellite Earth Station, is about 5 miles north-west along the B3293 – visitors are welcome.

Manacles Rocks – A favourite spot with divers visiting the many shipwrecks which the rocks have claimed. Many of the wreck victims lie in St Keverne's Churchyard.

REFRESHMENTS:

There are several cafés and an inn at Coverack, another inn at St Keverne and a restaurant at Porthoustock.

Walk 88   MEVAGISSEY AND GORRAN HAVEN   6$\frac{1}{2}$m (10km)

Maps: OS Sheets Landranger 204; Pathfinder 1361.

Fine cliff scenery and pleasant farmland paths, but some steep bits!

Start: At 014448, Mevagissey.

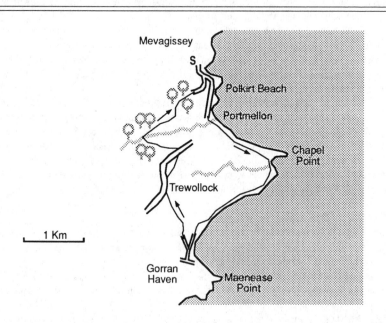

The walk commences in **Mevagissey**, which sits on the B3273, south of St Austell and should be explored for its many delightful features.

Take the road which leads steeply up from the inner harbour, heading westwards and following the helpful South West Coastal Path 'acorn' signs. Go past some fine houses to reach the suburb of Portmellon, continuing steeply up Chapel Point Lane. The lane goes between houses, then becomes a clear path offering good views left across the bay to Black Head and, further off, Gribbin Head. The white buildings of a school appear ahead: the path swings off to the right just before the entrance and descends to Coluna Beach. The South West Coastal Path is now followed for almost 2 miles, rising and falling and concluding by going through bushes and over stiles to reach the outskirts of **Gorran Haven** with its narrow lanes. To find the inn, turn right into Chute Lane. Alternatively, descend to the beach for light refreshments.

To return to Mevagissey, ascend the village street for a steep $^1/_2$ mile to reach a telephone kiosk at a junction of lanes. Turn right, and then left along Trewollock Lane. Turn right at the next junction, but soon go left, heading due north along a hedged lane for a short $^1/_2$ mile. Just after ignoring a left junction, turn right through a field gate with a footpath sign and follow the clear path beyond diagonally across two fields, heading north-north-eastwards to emerge on to a lane. Turn right, but very soon sharp left, westwards, along a track that goes steeply down to a stream and house.

Cross the stream and, keeping the house on your left, swing right to follow a rough track, with the stream off to the right. The track becomes indistinct and overgrown, so keep up to the left, walking along the bottom edge of a field. Go through a hedge gap and contour around to the left to reach Penwarne Farm. Go through the farm buildings, keeping the farmhouse below and off to the right. Go through a gate and follow the farm access track around to the right. This leads to an estate of bungalows above Portmellon. Do not descend: instead, turn left and then left again through the estate to reach a signpost, to the right, which indicates a footpath descending to the road just below the Harbour Lights Hotel. Now turn left and descend into Mevagissey.

POINTS OF INTEREST:

Mevagissey – A village of cottages grouped around a natural harbour. Once a busy fishing port, but more of a tourist attraction now. The church, dedicated to St Peter, was begun in the 13th century.

Gorran Haven – This was also once a pilchard-fishing port, but is now an attractive holiday resort with a fine beach.

Modern Cornish fishermen seek crabs and lobsters, trawl for cod, plaice and sole and go deeper and afar for the larger catch. Smaller boats are available for holiday-makers to try for mackerel etc.

REFRESHMENTS:

The Llawnroc Hotel, Gorran Haven (spell it backwards!).
There is a wide variety of cafés and restaurants in Mevagissey.

Walk 89   BUDE'S CANAL AND CLIFFS   6½m (10km)

Maps: OS Sheets Landranger 190; Pathfinder 1292.

Level walking along the Bude Canal at first, then a section of the South West Coastal Path.

Start: At 199032, the car park near Salthouse, to the north of Widemouth Bay.

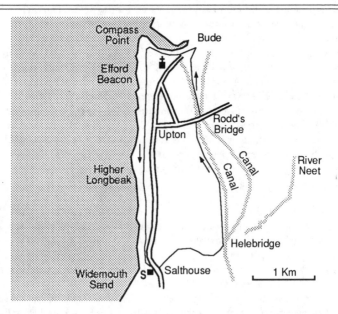

Leave the car park, which is located just north of Widemouth Bay, off the A39 about 4 miles south of the very popular resort of Bude, and walk south along the track to reach the converted old Salthouse. Obey the sign requesting that you 'take the path to the rear of cottage', then turn left, inland. Cross the road and go over the stile, following a sign 'to Helebridge'. Follow the hedge, to the left, heading generally eastwards. Go over several stiles, then diagonally across a field, soon descend to reach a road and Helebridge. The route turns left, northwards, now following the **Bude Canal** towpath for about a mile to reach Rodd's Bridge. Cross the canal here and turn left to continue along the other side. There is a hide here for quiet observation of the abundant wildlife.

Follow the towpath all the way into **Bude** where there are ample opportunities for rest and refreshment.

To continue, turn seawards, cross the bridge near the Falcon Hotel and go along the road to reach the church, on the left. Now, after passing some modern houses, look out for a gate and bridleway sign pointing westward. Follow the bridleway to reach the cliffs at the aptly named Compass Point. Note the octagonal building sited so that its walls point north, north-east, east etc., the eight major points of the Compass. The route is straightforward now, following the clear path southwards. Go past Efford Beacon and then down to Upton. Continue along the well-signed route towards Widemouth Sand, passing Philip's Point and Higher Longbeak before reaching the starting car park.

POINTS OF INTEREST:

The Bude Canal – The canal has had little commercial use for more than 100 years. Originally it was used mainly to transport lime and sea-sand inland to sweeten the acid soils of Cornish farms.

Bude – Justifiably popular as a seaside resort the town is a welcome halfway point for this walk. If you have the time, be sure to visit the interesting 'shipwreck' museum.

REFRESHMENTS:

There is something for everyone's taste in Bude.

Walk 90   FOWEY AND POLKERRIS   7m (11km)

Maps: OS Sheets Landranger 200, Pathfinder 1354.

Across farmland footpaths to a seaside cove, then a cliff path back to Fowey.

Start: At 110511, Readymoney Car Park, near Fowey.

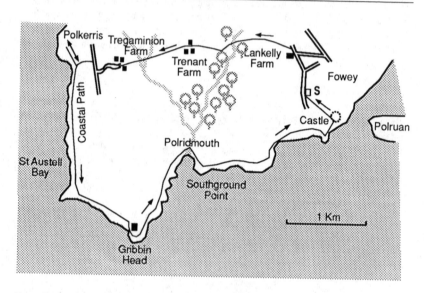

From the car park, which lies to the south-west of **Fowey**, walk back along the lane, heading northwards. Ignore the road going right, into Fowey, and after a short ½ mile turn left to follow the signed footpath by Lankelly Farm. The path leads downhill beside a barbed-wire fence, to the left, into a valley. Cross a stream and continue through trees. Now go over several stiles as you climb uphill, heading westwards to pass some old buildings. Go through Trenant Farm, beyond which more stiles are crossed as the path goes up, and then down to cross footbridges over two streams. Continue to reach Tregaminion Farm. Continue ahead, going through two gates to reach a lane. Turn right along the lane, then go left at a sign for 'Polkerris and Beach'. Walk downhill towards St Austell Bay.

For a visit to **Polkerris**, with its beach and refreshments, a short detour is necessary, following a path going to the right. The route continues by following a fine stretch of the South West Coastal Path, well marked with acorn signs. Go over several stiles and through a gate (which must be closed behind you) to reach the red-and-white tower at Gribbin Head. Now head eastwards towards Fowey ahead, going through several more gates and crossing stepping-stones when the sign for 'Lankelly Cliff' is followed. Continue over several stiles and through further gates, all the while enjoying the views, especially of the little coves carved from the coast. Follow signs for Coombe Haven and then for Alldays Fields to reach St Catherine's Castle.

On reaching the castle turn left, inland, northwards to return to the Readymoney car park.

POINTS OF INTEREST;
Fowey – An ancient port on the River Fowey and still very important for exporting china-clay to all parts of the world. Luckily the white dust-covered quays are $\frac{1}{2}$ mile upstream and away from the holiday town, which has literary associations with Quiller-Couch, Kenneth Grahame and Daphne Du Maurier. The town and its many narrow streets deserve a visit.
Polkerris – There is a delightful sandy beach here, as well as a small fishing quay and an Elizabethan pilchard cellar.

REFRESHMENTS:
The Ship Inn, Fowey.
The Lugger Inn, Fowey.
The Rashleigh Inn, Polkerris.
There is also an excellent tea-rooms in Polkerris.

Walk 91   MINIONS   7¹⁄₂m (12km)

Maps: OS sheets Landranger 201; Pathfinder 1339.

The remains of prehistoric man and more recent miners in a scenic landscape.

Start: At 262712, the village of Minions, north of Liskeard.

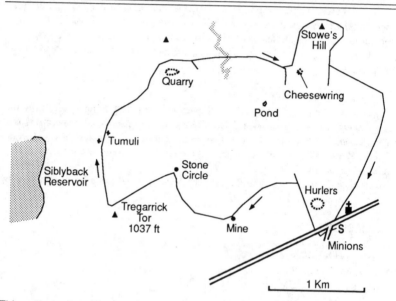

This walk requires a clear day, a compass and map (the Pathfinder is best) and some resolution. The directions indicate many opportunities to wander off to peruse the interesting relics of people of the past as well as to savour the scenery of Bodmin Moor.

Continue along the road, south-westwards from **Minions**, then turn right along the signposted track leading to **The Hurlers**. The stones are to the left of the track: after examining them, return to the track and continue northwards. After a further 200 yards, by more stones, bear left and head for the chimney and engine house of 'Silver Valley', heading west-south-westwards. On reaching the ruin, wander north-westwards to a stone circle, then go left again and cross to Tregarrick Tor – a good view point. The route continues due north now, passing many tumuli on the way to a

172

small summit by the pool, to the left, near the old granite quarry workings. Here turn east (right) – it may be boggy – to reach another pile of stones – a natural phenomenon known as **The Cheesewring** – on top of which carvings cut by an 18th-century astronomer can be seen. Better views can be obtained by turning north to the top of **Stowe's Hill** and then curving around south-east and then south along an old railway line that leads back to Minions.

POINTS OF INTEREST:

Minions – Standing at almost 1,000 feet above sea level, the village was once a busy centre concerned with local mining (for copper and tin) and granite quarrying.

The Hurlers – Reputed to be more than 3,500 years old and possibly the centre of ceremony and ritual, the local story is that the stones are men punished for playing ball-games on a Sunday!

The Cheesewring – The disc-like boulders balanced so precariously give the name, being reminiscent of a cider press, the local name for apple pulp being cheese. It is believed locally that the topmost stone revolves three times when it hears the cock crow!

Stowe's Hill – It has been suggested that the group of boulders on the summit are the remains of an Iron Age fort.

REFRESHMENTS:

The Cheesewring Inn, Minions.
The Post Office in Minions does excellent cream teas.

Walk 92   **POLPERRO AND LOOE**   8m (13km)

Maps: OS Sheets Landranger 201; Pathfinder 1355.
An easy, very scenic walk along the Coastal Path and quiet lanes.
Start: At 213510, the main car park, Polperro.

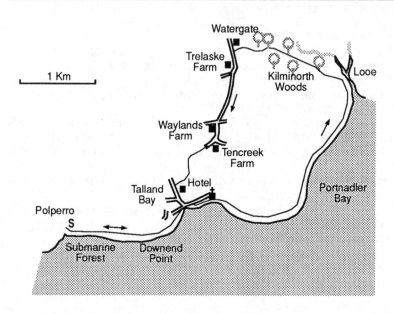

After enjoying the many captivating features of the village and harbour at **Polperro**
walk eastwards along the cliffs known as **The Warren** and descend, after a long mile,
to **Talland Bay** and its beach. Pass the public toilets, to the right, and then turn right,
following the road for about ¹/₄ mile before forking right on to the Coastal Path again.
Talland Church is off to the left at first. The walk continues along the clear Path for
another 3 miles into **Looe**.

Refreshments are available by turning right over the bridge. To continue, keep
the river on your right, go along the causeway and then head north-westward through
Kilminorth Woods. On reaching a map by a car park, keep ahead at a sign to a picnic
area, but soon fork left, ascending where there is a bench, to the right, and a bridleway
sign. After a further 150 yards, keep right along the main track and go through the

174

trees for a mile, heading westwards. Go through a gate into a lane, and turn left, uphill, passing a farm. At the fork, keep left (the right turn is private) and head southwards for about a mile to reach a crossing road (the A387).

Go straight over, with care, and follow the lane ahead (Wayland's Farm access) and, just before the lane swings left, take the right-hand lane by Tencreek Farm. Descend to a ford and bridge and go up the rougher track ahead, through a farmyard, to reach another road. Turn left along the road, going straight on at the next junction and then down to reach Talland Bay again. Now retrace the outward route along The Warren to return to Polperro.

POINTS OF INTEREST:

Polperro – This is everyone's idea of the typical Cornish fishing village – cameras essential – though despite being traffic-free, it is very commercialised. The tiny entrance to the harbour can be closed by heavy baulks of timber in stormy weather.

The Warren – This area of cliffs was once owned by Angela Brazil the novelist who bequeathed it to the National Trust.

Talland Bay – Note the beautifully coloured slates and, on approaching the river-mouth, Looe Island off-shore, on which, it is said, Joseph of Arimathea and Christ stayed.

Looe – East and West Looe are united by a bridge spanning two small rivers of the same names. There are good sandy beaches, boats for hire – shark fishing! – and the fine wooded area of Kilminorth.

REFRESHMENTS:

There is a good selection, for all tastes and pockets, in Polperro and Looe.

Walk 93   **BOTALLACK AND PENDEEN**   8m (13km)

Maps: OS Sheets Landranger 203; Pathfinder 1364.

A rugged cliff walk plus farmland and the scenery of our industrial past.

Start: At 391346, Bojewyan.

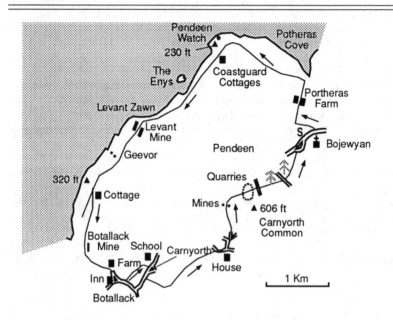

This rather demanding but very rewarding walk begins in the hamlet of Bojewyan on the B3306 between St Ives and St Just.

From the Men's Institute building, head north-eastwards for some 30 yards, then take a path on the left, opposite the chapel. Go over two stiles, along the left edge of a field and through a gap in a wall. Continue ahead across the next field and go through a second wall-gap to reach a lane. Turn right along the lane, for about ¹/₃ mile, to Portheras Farm. Turn right, then go between walls, through a gate and bear right towards a wall-corner. Maintaining the north-east direction, ignore a path going left, but after a further 50 yards, turn right. After another 50 yards, turn left, making for the sea. The Coastal Path is reached after another 250 yards: turn left and follow the acorn signs for 3 miles. The Pendeen Watch lighthouse is soon passed, as are coastguard cottages and the remains of the **Levant Mine**. Beyond, yellow waymarks offer a small detour to the Geevor Mine and, a $1/_2$ mile on, after passing a ruined cottage and as the Coastal Path forks right towards the cliffs, keep ahead (due south) to reach the ruins of the **Botallack Mine**. At a lane junction, to the right of Manor Farm, turn right and after about 30 yards, at the edge of Botallack village, turn left to reach the B3306.

Turn left along the road, then left again into a lane between cottages. Go over a stone stile and through three fields to emerge in Carnyorth village. At the grassy triangle just off to the right, turn right down the main road, but after 205 yards, just before coming to the back of the village sign, take the track off to the left. Ascend the track for about $1/_4$ mile and, on reaching a fork, go left between walls to reach the open country of Carnyorth Common. Head north-eastwards for $1/_2$ mile to reach a road (the B3318). Turn right, and, opposite a house, turn left. After 50 yards, at a fork, keep right, and after another 50 yards, fork left to descend towards chimneys and derelict mine buildings. Beyond, after yet another 50 yards, turn right, with a wall on your left, to go along the edge of the common. Go past quarries to reach a junction of tracks. Pendeen village is off to the left, but the walk continues over the stile ahead: go along a field edge, over another stile and, maintain direction to cross more stiles and fields to reach the B3318 again. Turn left, then immediately right through a gate. Go left along the left edge of a field and through the hedge-gap into the next field. Go along the left field edge again but, halfway along, in a gap in bushes, cross over a wall into a walled path which leads to a lane. Turn right and follow the lane round by cottages to reach a T-junction in Bojewyan where the Men's Institute is at hand.

POINTS OF INTEREST:

Levant Mine – This was working until 1930, the metal ore being extracted from tunnels 600 feet down and a mile out to sea.

Botallack Mine – You can visit, following in the footsteps of Queen Victoria and family who came in 1846. Both Levant and Botallack began as copper mines, but later yielded arsenic, tin and tungsten. The nearby Geevor Mine is still working.

REFRESHMENTS:

There are numerous possibilities in Botallack and Pendeen, and in nearby St Just and St Ives.

Walk 94   PORTREATH AND COOMBE   8m (13km)

Maps: OS Sheets Landranger 203; Pathfinder 1359.

Woods and coastal path. The walk can be boggy and is steep in places.

Start: At 658454, Portreath.

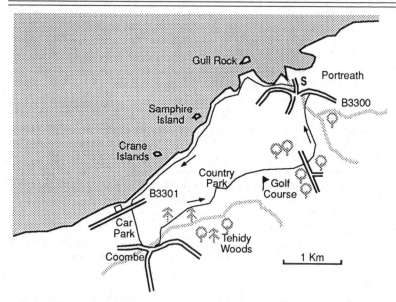

The directions for this walk are fairly simple – the scenery and woodland paths are fine – take the camera and the binoculars – and stout footwear.

Begin in the little port of **Portreath** and take the signed Coastal Path westwards and then south-westwards, with splendid sea views off to the right. Walkers might also be rewarded by a sighting of grey seals which frequent the rocky shoreline. Inland it is easy to spot the Dunstanville Monument near Redruth. Samphire Island is named after the succulent herbs which grow about the area, the leaves were once gathered for pickling.

About 3 miles from the start turn inland near a car park (at grid reference 624432) to reach the busy B3301. Cross, with great care, and go over a stile opposite to enter a field. Continue almost due south for $\frac{1}{2}$ mile to reach the hamlet of Coombe. There, turn left along a lane, but shortly go left again to enter Tehidy Woods. The track is clear through the woodland, heading eastwards for almost 2 miles. The trees cease for a short while as the path becomes gravelly and ascends, but soon reappears. Go past an old hospital and continue, finally emerging by an area of holiday chalets and a Country Park. Maintain the easterly course for another $1/_2$ mile to reach the edge of a golf course. Walk alongside the course and then descend to reach a farm and a minor road. Cross the road, then bear left, northwards, and descend a track to join the B3300. Turn left, with care, and follow the road back to start.

POINTS OF INTEREST:

Portreath – The local philanthropist Francis Basset de Dunstanville was instrumental in building the port facilities and harbour at Portreath so that locally mined copper ore could be handled easier than off the beach as it had been previously. The landmark 'The Pepperpot' by the pier was particularly useful in the stormy coastal conditions when Portreath was a very thriving harbour – the local population exceeded 30,000 in the early 1800s.

REFRESHMENTS:

There is nothing en route but there are various cafés, restaurants and inns in Portreath.

Walk 95   BOLVENTOR AND BROWN WILLY   8m (13km)

Maps: OS Sheets Landranger 201; Explorer 9.

A straight 'there and back' walk to the highest point in Cornwall.
Start: At 182768, the Jamaica Inn, Bolventor.

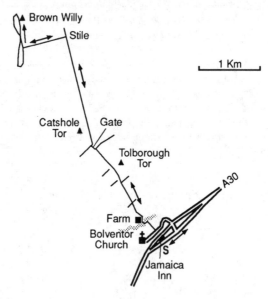

This walk is along permitted paths and official rights of way. It should only be attempted in clear weather. There are no refreshments en route.

From the **Jamaica Inn**, which sits to the side of the A30 near Bolventor, go under the main road and follow the access road signed for Bolventor Church, walking parallel to the main road for about 150 yards. Now take the signed footpath to the right (before reaching the church), going over stiles and following yellow and white markers downhill. The route bears left and crosses a little stream, then goes uphill to pass to the right of a farmhouse. Continue uphill along a rough and stony walled track to reach a gate. Go through and head north-north-westwards out on to open moorland. Maintain direction, passing to the left of Tolborough Tor. After a further $^{1}/_{4}$ mile descend to reach a gate near the junction of three fences.

Go through the gate and maintain the north-north-westward line uphill, with a grassy stone wall to your right and fence to your left, for a long mile. At first the clitters and outcrops of Catshole Tor are off to the left but after passing these Brown Willy and the ridge can be seen away to the left. The fence, to the left, is crossed by means of a stile when you are almost parallel to **Brown Willy**. Beyond, the route continues by heading due west across rough, and often boggy, grass, at first ascending gently, but ultimately very steeply. At the top a pause can be made to admire the extensive views (and to regain breath!) before turning right to reach the trig. point and the tor-top, at 1,378 feet. After spending time exploring the ridge, with its many strange rock formations and caves it is best not to risk the boggy conditions due south. Instead, return to the stile, cross and turn right to retrace the outward route back to Jamaica Inn.

POINTS OF INTEREST:

Jamaica Inn – Famous for Daphne du Maurier's story of smuggling and other infamous deeds, this was once a coaching inn providing much needed refreshment for travellers crossing the lonely moor. It still does. An additional, but optional extra, is the weird and bizarre museum of taxidermy and oddities at the adjacent 'Potter's Museum of Curiosity'.

Brown Willy – The peak's curious name derives from the Cornish *bron ewhella* which simply means highest hill. From the top the Stannon China Clay tips are clearly seen to the west, the Bristol Channel is due north, Colliford Lake is the large expanse of water to the south and, further off the English Channel.

REFRESHMENTS:

The Jamaica Inn, at the start.

Maps: OS Sheets Landranger 203; Pathfinder 1368.
Cliff path, prehistoric circles and a wooded valley.
Start: At 446245, the car park in Lamorna Cove.

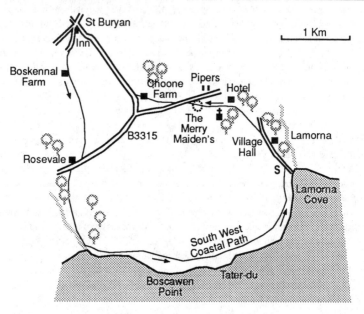

Follow the road leading up out of **Lamorna Cove**, passing the Wink Inn and the village hall. After a further 120 yards, fork left on to an ascending track, following it to reach a lane, with an hotel to the right. Maintain the westward course for a further ¹/₄ mile to reach a road junction. Turn left through a hedge gap just to the right of an hotel sign, and bear right across the field beyond to reach a stile in the hedge. Cross and go half-right through a stone circle – **The Merry Maidens** – to reach the B3315. Turn left for a few yards, then cross a stile on the right (it may be overgrown). Now take care – bear a little right to reach another stile, cross into the field and maintain direction to reach a third stile. Cross into another field and walk half-right to reach a fourth stile. Cross into the next field and after 15 yards, follow the path going left which descends through bushes towards Choone Farm. About 50 yards to the left of the farmhouse, go over a stile, cross the access road and go over another stile. Continue alongside a fence and as this bears off to the right, walk a little left to reach a gate on to a lane. Turn right and follow the lane for $1\frac{1}{2}$ miles into **St Buryan**.

Turn left beyond the village inn, into Boskennal Lane, and follow it for about 400 yards. When the lane turns right, go ahead, south-eastwards, then cross a stone stile and maintain direction for a further $1\frac{1}{2}$ miles (going through a farmyard, alongside a wall, over another stone stile, and alongside seven fields separated by stiles) to reach the B3315 again. Turn right and follow the road, with care, downhill. Now look out for a 'cattle' sign opposite 'Rosevale'. There, turn left through a gate and go through a wood (heading south-westward again) for a splendid $\frac{1}{4}$ mile of walking. Pass some houses and go over a stream, then turn left and, after a further 100 yards, cross yet another stile to join the Coastal Path. Now follow the Path, eastwards, for 2 miles, going along a beach and then up on to the cliffs which are followed all the way back to the start at Lamorna.

POINTS OF INTEREST:
Lamorna Cove – Delightful cottages, craft shops and artists' colony at the edge of the Lands End granite outcrop.
The Merry Maidens – The circle and the nearby standing stones of 'The Pipers' are but two of very many prehistoric stones which abound in Cornwall. Legend has it that the nineteen maidens danced on the Sabbath to the music of pipers and were all punished by being turned into stone.
St Buryan – The village's 14th-century granite church tower dominates much of the surrounding district. The six bells within are reputed to be the second heaviest in England. Note also a fine rood screen, a granite porch, a 17th-century slate tombstone and an unusual font.

REFRESHMENTS:
The Wink Inn, Lamorna.
The St Buryan Inn, St Buryan.

Walk 97   TREVOSE HEAD   9¹/₂m (15km)

Maps: OS Sheets Landranger 200; Pathfinder 1337.
Country lanes, footpaths and cliff coastline in North Cornwall.
Start: At 891759, the car park in Trevone, off B3276 west of
Padstow.

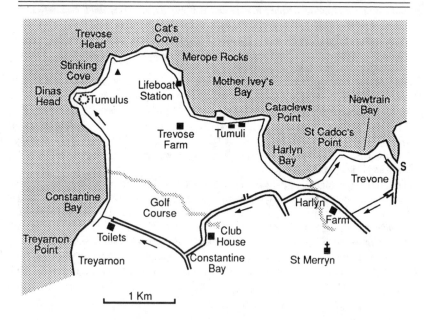

Choose a clear dry day for this rather strenuous walk.

From the **Trevone** car park take the road back towards the B3276 (southwards),
but turn right along Dobbin Lane, past Pol's Piece, and continue along a rough track.
Go over a metal and brick stile into a field – St Merryn's church tower is a distant
landmark – and cross to reach a road. Turn right, back towards the sea, walking through
the hamlet of **Harlyn**. At the road fork, take the left branch to ascend away from the
bay. Turn right at the next junction, and shortly after the left-hand bend keep ahead,
south westwards, along the road, ignoring the signed track 'To Trevose Head'.

Stay on the lane, passing a golf course, to the right, to reach a footpath signed
'Constantine Bay', also to the right. Follow this path around the links and down to

the sands. (A short detour left here will enable walkers to sample refreshments in Treyarnon.) The route continues by turning right along the beach and climbing the rocks at the end to reach the Coastal Path. Follow the Path, generally northwards, around Constantine Bay, Booby's Bay, Dinas Head and the oddly named Stinking Cove to reach the lighthouse at **Trevose Head**.

The walk continues round Mother Ivey's Bay and Cataclews Point, where the sands of Harlyn Bay come into view. Descend to the beach (refreshments again!) and then ascend St Cadoc's Point. Now go down to Newtrain Bay, then go along field edges and over a stile. Walk along another field edge and continue to reach the beach at Trevone. Turn right into the village and the starting point.

POINTS OF INTEREST:

Trevone – Note the chapel's slate spire, the fine sandy beach and the caves and arches between the village and Trevose Head.

Harlyn – There is a little museum here with a collection of artefacts excavated from a nearby Celtic burial ground.

Trevose Head – Reaching 243 feet above the sea, this headland is a splendid viewpoint with towering rocks, rocky islets, steep cliffs and flocks of sea-birds. At night four lighthouses are visible. The natural rock-arches, rocky reefs and tempting little beaches along the local coast make this a fascinating walking area.

REFRESHMENTS:

The Well Parc Hotel, Trevone.

The Harlyn Inn, Harlyn Bay.

There are also restaurants in Trevone, and the detour mentioned in the text to Treyarnon Hotel, Treyarnon.

Walk 98   CASTLE-AN-DINAS   11m (17$\frac{1}{2}$km)

Maps: OS Sheets Landranger 200; Pathfinder 1346.

Lanes, tracks and an Iron Age fort. Some traffic!

Start: At 945621, the car park at Castle-an-Dinas.

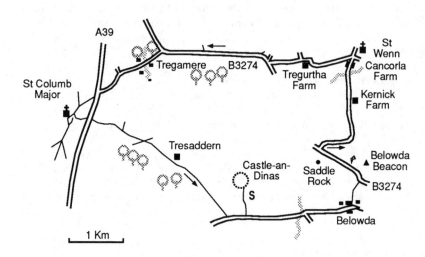

This longer, sometimes muddy, but rewarding, walk commences at the car park by **Castle-an-Dinas** about 3 miles east of St Columb Major, which is on the A39 about 9 miles south-west of Wadebridge.

After exploring the fort, turn south down the footpath back to the approach road. Taking great care, turn left for $\frac{1}{2}$ mile, forking left at the bottom of the hill to continue along a quieter lane into the hamlet of Belowda. Again fork left, this time along a clear footpath, following it for $\frac{1}{4}$ mile to join the B3274. Turn left, again with great care, and follow the road downhill, with Belowda Beacon off to the right and, soon, Saddle Rock to the left. After a short $\frac{1}{2}$ mile, take the lane on the right, to Kernick. This runs due east at first, then swings left (northwards) passing the farm and then going over the bridge. Go past Lancorla Farm and maintain direction to reach a crossroads. Ahead is the hamlet of St Wenn.

The walk continues by turning left along a lane heading westwards. Go past Tregurtha Farm and continue to reach the B3274 at a bend. Follow, with great care, this road, which is signed to Padstow, for a mile, enjoying the many fine views and ignoring a turning to the right. When a turn to the left (forming a fork) is reached, take this lane, which is signed to Tregamere. Follow the lane south-westwards through the hamlet of Tregamere. Bear left at a junction of lanes and continue, going under the A39, and on into **St Columb Major** – the church tower is an excellent guide ahead. Go uphill into the town – you are now walking south. At Barclays Bank, go left into Broad Street, and right down the hill. At the bottom, go through a gate and ascend to reach the town's by-pass, the A39. Cross, with great care, and follow the lane signed to Tregatillian. Ignore lanes with signs to Trenillocs and Trevithick, maintaining direction when a road comes in from the right to reach a fork. Take the right branch to pass the old mill and the farm at Tresaddern, continuing to reach a Y-junction. Bear left, with care, at this busy junction and then turn left to return to the start.

POINTS OF INTEREST:
Castle-an-Dinas – This splendid viewpoint (given a clear day) is claimed to be the birthplace of King Arthur. It is almost certainly an Iron Age hill-fort, founded more than 3,800 years ago.
St Columb Major – An old market town with the 15th-century church dedicated to St Columba, containing carved bench ends, fine brasses and modern wood, bronze and glass work.

REFRESHMENTS:
There is a wide choice in St Columb Major.

Walk 99   ALTARNUN AND JAMAICA INN $11^1/_2$m (18km)

Maps: OS Sheets Landranger 201; Pathfinders 1338 and 1339.
A long, but fairly easy, walk – moorland, forest and farmland.
Start: At 223813, Altarnun Church.

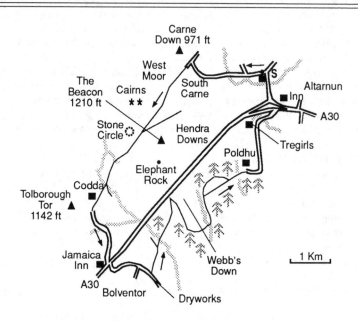

This long walk is straightforward, but does require careful navigation, good footwear, clear visibility and fitness as it covers almost 12 miles of Bodmin Moor. The rewards are great – a lonely landscape, coniferous forest and a 'special' inn and museum.

From the church in **Altarnun**, dedicated to Saint Non – the mother of Saint David – take the lane signposted to South Carne. This ascends steeply at first, then goes down and then up again, heading generally westward to reach, after about $1^1/_2$ miles, the straggly hamlet itself. Follow the road past the last buildings: the road turns northwards and, further on, bends right (north-eastwards). Here, turn left through a gate, heading south-westwards along a high-banked track on to West Moor.

The route continues south-westwards for $3^1/_2$ miles, heading for the farm at Codda with the summit of Tolborough Tor behind it. There are cairns off to the right; a track

188

coming in from the left; The Beacon (1210 feet – 369m), also to the left; and a stone circle just off to the right, as the way leads gently downhill to cross the infant River Fowey (waymarks assist!). Continue to reach a little bridge and Codda. Now turn southwards for another mile, following a lane past Blackadon Farm and Tolborough to reach **Bolventor** and the Jamaica Inn.

Having crossed under the trunk road (the A30), proceed eastwards along the road signed for St Cleer for about $^1/_2$ mile, then turn left at Dryworks, following a track signed for Webb's Down. This track becomes stony as it descends to the River Fowey. Cross the bridge over the river and climb north-eastwards back towards the A30 once more. On arriving at a lane which goes under the A30, turn right (ie. do not go under the main road) and follow the lane for $^1/_2$ mile to reach a conifer plantation. A few hundred yards into the forest, bear left along a clear, stony track. Follow this for $^1/_4$ mile, then go left again, heading northwards. After another $^1/_4$ mile, bear right along a grassy track to leave the forest. Now follow a lane, passing Poldhu Farm. The lane turns sharply left, due north, to pass Tregirls, then goes under the A30 and returns to Altarnun and the start of the walk.

POINTS OF INTEREST:

Altarnun – An ancient hump-backed bridge; the 15th-century church of St Nonna (or Non) with fascinating bench-ends depicting bagpipes, fiddles and a village idiot etc; and stone cottages, make this village a place to savour.

Bolventor – Time must be made to visit the Museum of Mr Potter's and its many curiosities as well as the extra attractions in the Jamaica Inn.

REFRESHMENTS:

It might be useful to have a snack and flask for the journey to Bolventor where the Jamaica Inn will provide traditional fare – and perhaps another snack before arriving back at Altarnun and its further refreshing opportunities.

Walk 100   ZENNOR AND ST IVES   12m (19km)

Maps: OS Sheets Landranger 203; Explorer 7.

A full-day walk: lovely granite walls, farms linked by an ancient 'way' and superb cliff-walking.

Start: At 454384, Zennor Church.

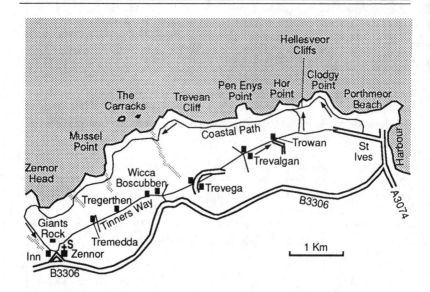

This all-day walk takes the walker along the old Tinners Way across granite-walled farmland for about $4\frac{1}{2}$ miles then heads due north to the sea, before turning west along the South West Coastal Path to the numerous interests and refreshments of St Ives.

From the church, dedicated to St Senara, in **Zennor** cross the cattle grid in the churchyard's north-west corner, then go right (east-north-eastwards), following a clear path across the fields to Tremedda. There, go over a crossing track and maintain direction to Tregerthen. Pass the farm buildings, to the left, and keep straight on to Boscubben. Having passed the farm, go left for about 50 yards, then right, over a stile. Now maintain direction to pick up the black and white markers of the Tinners Way, following it through Trendrine and Trevessa farms to reach a lane.

Go left, and immediately right at Trevega. Continue to reach the lane once more. Go right, still following Tinners Way signs, soon bearing left towards Trevalgan. Keep the farm off to your right and walk ahead for a further $1/4$ mile to reach Trowan. Still maintaining the same direction, continue along a short $1/2$ mile of farm track to reach a path crossing. Keep ahead for a further $1/4$ mile to join a road at a junction. Turn right, downhill, into **St Ives**, with its artists colony, museum, picturesque harbour and wide range of refreshments.

To continue the walk, leave the harbour and attractive Porthmeor Beach and follow the Cornish Coastal Path, part of the South West Coastal Path, heading westwards to Clodgy Point. Continue westward to Hellesveor Cliffs from where you should look back to enjoy the superb views eastwards to Godrevy Point and beyond. On this section of the walk you should also look out for kittiwakes and seals above and below the cliff edge, but do take care as the path seems suspended between earth and sky!

Cross three streams as you follow the Path a little south of west and, about 3 miles from Hellesveor, go around Zennor Head before turning left, inland, along a lane leading back to Zennor.

POINTS OF INTEREST:
Zennor – The church of St Senara has a Mermaid Chair which is part of the famous Mermaid legend. Do not miss a visit to the little museum with its collection of old Cornish farm implements, cottage tools etc.

St Ives – A justly famous resort with two fine museums, a much-photographed and painted harbour and a wide variety of refreshments.

REFRESHMENTS:
There is a wide variety of possibilities in St Ives, and an inn at the start in Zennor.

TITLES IN THE SERIES

Cheshire

County Durham

Derbyshire

Devon and Cornwall

Dorset

Essex

Gloucestershire

Hampshire & the Isle of Wight

Hereford and Worcester

Kent

Lancashire

Northumberland

Somerset and Avon

Staffordshire

Surrey

East Sussex

West Sussex

Warwickshire & the West Midlands

Wiltshire

Yorkshire (Vols 1 and 2)